The Heritage of Literature Series

SMEDDUM

The Heritage of Literature Series

Founder General Editor: E.W. Parker, M.C.

The titles in this series include modern classics, and a wide range of novels, short stories and drama

A selection from the series includes

SUNSET SONG   *Lewis Grassic Gibbon*
GREENVOE   *George Mackay Brown*
WITCH AND OTHER STORIES   *George Mackay Brown*
ANIMAL FARM   *George Orwell*
THE WESKER TRILOGY   *Arnold Wesker*
GO TELL IT ON THE MOUNTAIN   *James Baldwin*
THE ROYAL HUNT OF THE SUN   *Peter Shaffer*
CRY, THE BELOVED COUNTRY   *Alan Paton*
FARMER'S BOY   *John R. Allan*
MISTER JOHNSON   *Joyce Cary*
BRAVE NEW WORLD   *Aldous Huxley*

A complete list of the series is available on request

SMEDDUM
Stories and Essays

LEWIS GRASSIC GIBBON

with commentary and notes by
D.M. BUDGE

LONGMAN

LONGMAN GROUP LIMITED
London
*Associated companies, branches and
representatives throughout the world*

These stories and essays previously published by Hutchinson
Publishing Group Limited in *A Scots Hairst* 1967
This edition first published by Longman Group Limited by
arrangement with the Hutchinson Publishing Group Limited 1980

ISBN 0 582 33070 x

Printed in Hong Kong by
Commonwealth Printing Press Ltd

CONTENTS

Commentary   vii
Note on the Texts   xvii

STORIES

Smeddum   1
Greenden   12
Sim   24
Forsaken   36
Clay   47

ESSAYS

The Antique Scene   61
Glasgow   80
Literary Lights   92
The Land   106

Select Bibliography of Mitchell's Works   121
Notes   122
Glossary   138

ACKNOWLEDGEMENTS

I should like to thank M.A. Begg, of the National Library of Scotland, for his willing assistance and many kindnesses. For the principal details of James Leslie Mitchell's life and career I am indebted to Ian S. Munro's admirable first biography *Leslie Mitchell : Lewis Grassic Gibbon* (1966).

COMMENTARY

The county of Kincardine is situated in the north-east of Scotland. The sea forms the eastern boundary, the Grampian Mountains lie to the west, and it is bounded on the north and south by the farming counties of Aberdeen and Angus. With the exception of the fishing communities on the seaboard, it is a county of small villages and numerous farms.

Although the modern county takes its name from Kincardine in the parish of Fordoun, the old name for the area was the Mearns and that term is still used widely in a place where people live and work on land which has seen little of change since the beginnings of history.

Men came to what is now Scotland some six to eight thousand years ago. They lived by gathering, hunting and fishing until the first farmers arrived from Europe with seed and stock and the practice of agriculture began. Other colonists were to follow, among them the Beaker Folk from Holland and the Rhineland who settled on Scotland's east coast.

From the mixed racial and cultural backgrounds of the various colonists a number of tribes evolved who were eventually given the collective name of Picts by the Romans. The Picts were sorely troubled by the Romans as they were later by the Scots and Vikings, but they survived until 840 when their last king was defeated by Kenneth MacAlpin and the lands of the Picts were united with the lands acquired by the invaders from Ireland called Scots. From that date the Picts as a political entity disappeared from the face of the earth. But their descendants, traces of their culture and their sculptured stones remain in modern Kincardine, and elsewhere in erstwhile Pictland, to this day.

Apart from the fisherfolk on the coast, the history of the

people of Kincardine is inextricably bound up with the history of the land. A coastal corridor providing a path for armies, traders and travellers, Kincardine was little disturbed by the passage of time and nothing arose in the area even remotely like the cities of Aberdeen in the north and Dundee in the south. Only one of history's changes markedly affected Kincardine, and that was the Agricultural Revolution.

Among the bogs, moors and stones of the Mearns people had scraped a living for countless years, but it was not until the middle of the eighteenth century that the first attempts at agricultural improvement were made and the long, back-breaking labour that was finally to shape the Kincardine of today began. Among the pioneers was a local landowner who imported a number of ploughmen from Norfolk to set a pace and show the way.

Gradually the uprooting of whins and heather, the draining of bogs, the clearing of stones, the building of walls and the planting of windbreaks brought the fertile acres to the fore, and by the beginning of this century Kincardine was comfortable in oats and barley, turnips and hay, with grass and pasture for its blackfaced sheep, cattle and Clydesdale horses. The Mearns presented a clean and tidy face yet the past endured, and there remained among the crofts and farms the stone circles and standing stones of the people who had lived there long ago.

In 1909 the Mitchell family moved into the farm-croft of Bloomfield above Arbuthnott in Kincardine. They had come after a short stay in Aberdeen from a not dissimilar landscape at Hillhead of Seggat, Auchterless, Aberdeenshire, where the third child, James Leslie, had been born in 1901. James Leslie Mitchell attended the local school and later went, a promising pupil, to Mackie Academy in Stonehaven, Kincardine's county town. For pupil and staff his time there was not a happy one and at the age of fifteen he left. In Aberdeen he found work on the *Aberdeen Daily Journal* and membership of the council of the Aberdeen Soviet. He later went south to Glasgow to work on the *Scottish Farmer* but there the cloud that had shadowed him at Mackie Academy returned and he was sacked. Shortly afterwards he joined the army and later the Royal Air Force. His first book, *Hanno: or the Future of Exploration: an Essay in Prophecy* (1928), had been published before he left the Royal Air Force in 1929 to become a professional writer. During the next five years he published sixteen books and many short stories and essays. In Welwyn Garden City in 1935, one week before his thirty-fourth birthday, he underwent an operation for a perforated gastric ulcer and died of peritonitis.

His early death removed from the world of books a writer whose biographical and archaeological work had reached high standards. In the field of fiction his novels appeared beside those of Ivy Compton-Burnett, Louis Golding, Charles Graves, Neil Gunn, James Hilton, Aldous Huxley, D.H. Lawrence, Somerset Maugham, J.B. Priestley, Evelyn Waugh and Virginia Woolf, to name but a few. The years 1928–34 were fertile ones in literary terms and Mitchell was one of many competent working writers ploughing a well-tilled field. His survival, his fame, and his niche in the annals of literature under his pseudynom of Lewis Grassic Gibbon, rest on the trilogy *A Scots Quair* (1946) and in particular on its first part, *Sunset Song* (1932).

Although *Sunset Song* has become the sacred cow of twentieth-century Scottish literature, and its author has been dead for over forty years, neither Mitchell's memory nor his work have inspired universal love and respect among the people of the Mearns. Even today there are those who regard him as a betrayer of the people of the north-east of Scotland. Not only was he the man who kissed and told, but he peered under stones and lifted hems. Worst of all, he wrote down what he saw and grievously disturbed the peace of some of his fellow countrymen.

Thirty-one years before him George Douglas Brown had done much the same damage to the genteel conceits of the villagers of Ayrshire in his novel *The House with the Green Shutters* (1910). Time has translated George Douglas Brown from one-time muck-raker into respectable citizen, but there is yet enough residual resentment in the Mearns to deny James Leslie Mitchell posthumous comfort.

More seriously, Mitchell has twice been accused of plagiarism. In 1962 it was suggested that *Sunset Song* was derived from Gustav Frenssen's *Jörn Uhl* which first appeared in the year of Mitchell's birth (Frederick Sefton Delmer's translation of the German Lutheran minister's novel was published in London in 1905). In 1975 the view was put forward that a book published one year before Mitchell's novel, *Shepherd's Calendar* by Ian MacPherson (another former pupil of Mackie Academy), was the true source of *Sunset Song*. Mitchell may, or may not, have read either or both books and he may, or may not, have been guilty of plagiarism. But where inspiration and influence end and where plagiarism begins is a matter sometimes best left to the judgement of a Solomon. What is certain is that Mitchell wrote a better book than either of those he may or may not have plagiarised.

That the charges of plagiarism are contemporary is confirmation that Mitchell has yet to achieve total respectability and that the bone-pickers are not yet finished with him. In an age when literature is often regarded as a rag-bag to be searched for manifestations of this or that political creed, Mitchell's work does not readily lend itself to dogma. Like Hugh MacDiarmid, his collaborator in *Scottish Scene or The Intelligent Man's Guide to Albyn* (1934), Mitchell defies any clear-cut and cosy classification.

In its early, heady days in Scotland Mitchell firmly embraced Communism. He was elected to the council of the Aberdeen Soviet in 1917, the year when the Bolshevik Revolution in Russia appeared to herald at last the beginning of the end of the workers' struggle. The revolution fired the imagination of the communists and in Scotland 'Red Clydeside' deepened its hue. The Bolsheviks appointed John Maclean Soviet Consul in Great Britain and Mitchell arrived to work in Glasgow only two months after an attempt had been made to turn that city's

Trades Council into a working soviet. What Mitchell saw of
the industrial unrest and dreadful living conditions in Glasgow
served to confirm him in his views. He later based his essay
'Glasgow' on memories of his five months' stay there, and he
looked back without mercy.

Mitchell left Glasgow in the summer of 1919 to end up, after
a few sad weeks at his Arbuthnott home, a soldier in Mesopo-
tamia. He left behind him a lively Scottish political scene as
the Communist, Labour, Liberal and Unionist parties fought
and squabbled. But at the rear of the British factions another
movement was finding a new lease of life. Between the end of the
Great War and Mitchell's death in 1935 some seventeen
assorted periodicals sympathetic to Scottish Nationalism rose
and fell, or occasionally survived.

Communists, ever international in outlook, rejected nationalism. Mitchell's opinion of nationalism was unequivocal and
vicious ('archaic ape-spite, a brosy barbarization'). He never
again returned to Scotland for any length of time, taking up
residence in England after leaving the Royal Air Force, his
communism perhaps strengthened by the poverty of his early
writing days. Towards the end of his life, his commitment to
communism apparently undiminished, his opposition to nationalism appeared to have eased and he had contributed on
several occasions to the Scottish Nationalist periodical *The Free
Man*.

To his early belief in Communism Mitchell soon grafted on
diffusionism. Diffusionist theories presented the attractive idea
of primitive man as an innocent, a contented roamer, kind
and happy, and without any sense of sin. He lived free of
government, and knew nothing of political or economic insti-
tutions, in an Eden that knew nothing of religion. His idyllic
way of life came to an end with a chance observation on the
banks of the Nile. There the annual flooding of that great
river coincided with the seasonal growth of wild barley and
within days of the water draining away young plants would
appear in the ground. When the thought of preserving the

wild seed and emulating the effects of the flooding by irrigating the land occurred to primitive man he had discovered agriculture, but the produce of his barley seed was to be accompanied by the weeds of civilisation.

Farming provided a constant supply of food and man no longer needed to roam. Communities grew up around the food stocks and soon required systems of government. The governments produced administrators and class distinctions began to emerge. Administrators planned the agriculture and a working class carried out their plans. From governments arose kings, from kings arose religions. From a chance observation on the banks of the Nile what is known as civilisation was diffused throughout the world. On the premise that civilisation was a mere accident of history the diffusionists based their creed and held that the true human condition is that of man in his Golden Age.

Mitchell seems to have yearned for a new Golden Age and thought communism a way of achieving it. While his self-acknowledged peasant nature and reverence for the peoples of the past were primary influences, his diffusionism and communism fired and moved much of his work. Although the diffusionists like the communists rejected nationalism, seeing it as yet another unpleasant by-product of civilisation, the two philosophies were incompatible. While both contributed in no small measure to *A Scots Quair* it was Mitchell's intuitive understanding of the land and the peasant and his passionate concern for humanity which lifted *Sunset Song* out of the Mearns, out of Scotland, and into the world. He presented in a fresh and fluent prose a painful probing into fundamental human values. Little wonder that his ashes have yet to find their peace.

Before the last book of *A Scots Quair* had been completed Mitchell joined with Hugh MacDiarmid in *Scottish Scene* to produce an exciting, rumbustious and irreverent book on Scotland and the Scots, with blows and sideswipes in all directions. Partly a reckless exercise in enemy-baiting, the miscellany rejoiced in sure vision untroubled by doubts, the modest arrogance of knowing most of the answers, and the exuberance of two writers ready and willing to take on all and sundry. Although they held opposing views on many matters and often contradicted each other, Mitchell and MacDiarmid were a well-matched pair for the venture. Both grabbed with gusto the opportunities offered in the concept of *Scottish Scene* and it was a literary tragedy that only MacDiarmid was to go on through the years to a ripe old age, merrily bewitching and bamboozling on his way.

Christopher Murray Grieve, man of many aliases, was already practised in the habit of reviewing in print his Hugh MacDiarmid work under his own name when Mitchell, not very seriously, similarly indulged himself in *Scottish Scene*. He wrote that Lewis Grassic Gibbon's technique in *A Scots Quair* was 'to mould the English language into the rhythms and cadences of Scots spoken speech, and to inject into the English vocabulary such minimum number of words from Braid Scots as that re-modelling requires'. Although he went on to question whether the technique would prove adequate, he had already employed it with total success in four of his five Scottish short stories. Two of those stories, 'Clay' and 'Smeddum', his essay 'The Land' and *Sunset Song* are Mitchell's greatest and enduring achievements.

In *Scottish Scene* 'Forsaken' made its first appearance, joining 'Sim' (originally published in *The Free Man*) and the three other stories which had appeared previously in *The Scots Magazine*. 'Forsaken' is the least successful of the group, its theme stilted and bordering on the queasy, a parable of Christ returning to earth and finding shelter with a communist family in a city with the largest Jewish community in Scotland. 'Greenden' is also a parable, but one of diffusionism in which Ellen's part in a complex tragedy is that of a survivor from a Golden Age slowly suffocating in the symbolic growth of civilisation and eventually driven to suicide, leaving behind her husband to thrive in an environment her innocence could not abide.

'Sim' is a character study of a man who ruthlessly reaches towards the milestones of his life and finds each in turn worthless. The story shows a rare understanding of a ploughman's mind and the harshness of an attitude to life, amounting at times to brutality, which can be found among some of the peasant stock of north-east Scotland and elsewhere. Sharply drawn, Sim Wilson is a grim individual, hell-bent down a hard road, yet even his singleminded drive and vigour seem almost pale when set beside the rich vitality of mighty Meg Menzies in 'Smeddum'.

Scottish literature has produced little in the way of heroines and of a meagre and lonely group two are the inspired work of James Leslie Mitchell – Chris Guthrie in *A Scots Quair* and Meg Menzies. Chris is a sweet and gentle creature, but Meg shatters the archetypal mould of conventional womanhood and goes forth in fear of neither God nor man. 'Smeddum' has deservedly long been the most popular of Mitchell's stories, a tale of rich humour where the spirit triumphs and the righteous are brought miserably to heel. Using the idiomatic fluency of *Sunset Song* the story is written with a deft authority which brings Meg Menzies brilliantly and vigorously alive. Of all James Leslie Mitchell's creations, Meg Menzies of Tocherty toun is the least likely to be forgotten.

While 'Smeddum' is a beautifully extended anecdote celebrating peasant spirit, 'Clay' is an ambitious piece demonstrating the diffusionist view that man has been enslaved by agriculture. Demeaned by the demands of the land, a decent human being becomes obsessed and then destroyed. Yet Mitchell's belief that man's salvation lies in some form of a return to nature provides the optimism of the final paragraph where Rachael, her father's corpse hardly cold, sees a different earth – an earth 'unquieted no longer'. 'Clay' owes little to communism and a great deal to diffusionism but, above all, it exemplifies Mitchell's impeccable understanding of the peasant and the land and the effects of their interaction. 'Clay' embodies the best of James Leslie Mitchell and is equalled only by his essay 'The Land'.

In *Scottish Scene* the work was evenly divided and of its fourteen essays, sketches and studies Mitchell contributed half. He lambasted religion in general and Scottish Presbyterianism in particular; presented a prose-assassination of James Ramsay MacDonald, prime minister of Britain's first Labour government; took an emotional look at Aberdeen and Glasgow; reviewed Scottish history and turned with unerring skill to the subject of the land.

In 'The Antique Scene' Mitchell offered a diffusionist view of Scottish history in an essay that in part reflected the Prelude of *Sunset Song*. He took up his beloved theme of the early peoples of Scotland, their Pictish descendants and their subsequent degradation. In such a short piece his encapsulation of history could not be other than over-simplified, but he expressed his interpretations with panache and managed a charitable word for John Knox in the by-going. He left charity behind in his sketch 'Glasgow' where memories of his time there rose like bile. In 'Aberdeen' his memories were partly autobiographical; he treated the city kindly and with affection in a backward look largely free of grief.

In 'Literary Lights' he demonstrated his belief in the non-existence of contemporary Scottish writers yielding a specifically Scottish literature. However he admitted to two possibilities in Hugh MacDiarmid and Lewis Spence and in a modest reference suggested that Lewis Grassic Gibbon might prove a further possibility. At the end of his essay he sensibly sidestepped the alien matter of Scottish Gaelic writing by quoting James Barke. Mitchell's wisdom in avoiding the subject was sadly confirmed in his unfortunate choice of quotation (p. 104). Barke, in his roll-call of the great, apparently did not realise that Alasdair MacMhaighistir Alasdair and Alexander MacDonald were one and the same person.

That Mitchell's best work is firmly rooted in the places of his childhood is clearly shown in his essay 'The Land'. It is a deeply felt and unromantic exposition of the land and of 'the men who conquered the land and wrung sustenance from it by stealth and shrewdness and a savage and surly endurance'. Mitchell's intense understanding of the nature of the land and what it means to the men and women who work on it took him far beyond the merely personal and particular to the universal. No other essay in *Scottish Scene* matched its brilliance and 'The Land' is, in its bitter-sweet perfection, definitive.

The landscapes of his childhood and early youth gripped Mitchell's mind and never left it, nor did a haunting feeling for the early peoples of Scotland and their strange standing stones ever desert him. His times in Aberdeen and Glasgow, the places abroad he saw as a serviceman, his devotion to communism and diffusionsim all served him for better or worse in his writing. But the best of his work took him back to Kincardine, to the land. All the 'isms' of his beliefs, all the overtones and allegories of his writing become subordinate to the passionate and mystic understanding of a peasant writer who looked back over the crofts and farms of the Mearns, through contemporary and recent Scottish history and over the culture of the Scottish Gaels, to the Picts and beyond. He proclaimed himself a true descendant of the Venricones and he served their shades triumphantly in his evocations of the land of their travail.

Even for a professional writer fully committed to his craft the year that saw the appearance of 'The Land' and Mitchell's other essays and stories in *Scottish Scene* was one of rich harvest. It started with publication of his biography *Niger: the Life of Mungo Park* and *The Conquest of the Maya*, followed by the novel *Gay Hunter* and, in the summer, *Scottish Scene*. Towards the end of the year, under the confusing authorship of 'J. Leslie Mitchell and Lewis Grassic Gibbon', came a collection of short biographies, *Nine Against the Unknown*, and *Grey Granite*, the third and final part of *A Scots Quair*. Three months later, in Queen Victoria Hospital, Welwyn Garden City, James Leslie Mitchell lay dead.

NOTE ON THE TEXTS

The story 'Forsaken' and the essays, sketches and studies by James Leslie Mitchell in *Scottish Scene* (1934) appeared there for the first time. The stories 'Greenden', 'Smeddum' and 'Clay' had been published previously in *The Scots Magazine* (1932–3) and 'Sim' in *The Free Man* (1933).

The four stories reprinted in *Scottish Scene* and later in *A Scots Hairst* (1967) were revised versions. 'Greenden', 'Smeddum' and 'Clay' had been shortened marginally by a few words; occasionally a single sentence replaced what had been two, here and there a word or phrase had been altered, and each story had shed commas. Similarly 'Sim' had fewer commas but, apart from the presentation of conversation in italics instead of quotation-marks, the changes were minute.

Ian S. Munro has told in his biography *Leslie Mitchell : Lewis Grassic Gibbon* (1966) how Mitchell immediately objected when 'Greenden' appeared in *The Scots Magazine* with the conversation in quotation-marks. The magazine's editor apologised and promised in future to follow Mitchell's manuscripts 'for punctuation and italics'. The style that Mitchell had established in *Sunset Song* was the hallmark of his Scottish fiction and he rightly regarded it as being of prime importance. There is therefore something strange about the publication in *The Free Man* of 'Sim' with the conversation in quotation-marks.

'Sim' was published seven months after Mitchell had remonstrated with the editor of *The Scots Magazine* and five months after the third of his Scottish stories had appeared in that magazine. The story is one of indisputable quality and might reasonably have been expected to follow the other three in *The Scots Magazine*. Although he had already contributed to it, *The Free Man* was a Scottish Nationalist periodical commanding a different and smaller readership – a fact of which the highly professional Mitchell would be well aware.

Furthermore it seems unlikely that, whatever the reason for the story's publication in *The Free Man*, Mitchell's manuscript would not have indicated his insistence upon italics instead of quotation-marks. Perhaps the editor of *The Free Man* decided to go his own way and follow convention, but Mitchell made certain of the italics when 'Sim' re-appeared in *Scottish Scene*.

While the texts in this edition are those of the primary sources the reader should bear in mind that Mitchell intended 'Greenden' (and, in all probability, 'Sim') to be presented in the same fashion as 'Smeddum', 'Clay' and 'Forsaken'.

STORIES

SMEDDUM

She'd had nine of a family in her time, Mistress Menzies, and brought the nine of them up, forbye – some near by the scruff of the neck, you would say. They were sniftering and weakly, two-three of the bairns, sniftering in their cradles to get into their coffins; but she'd shake them to life and dose them with salts and feed them up till they couldn't but live. And she'd plonk one down – finishing the wiping of the creature's neb or unco dosing of an ill bit stomach or the binding up of a broken head – with a look on her face as much as to say *Die on me now and see what you'll get!*

Big-boned she was by her fortieth year, like a big roan mare, and *If ever she was bonny 'twas in Noah's time,* Jock Menzies, her eldest son, would say. She'd reddish hair and a high, sheugh nose, and a hand that skelped her way through life; and if ever a soul had seen her at rest when the dark was done and the day was come he'd died of the shock and never let on.

For from morn till night she was at it, work, work, on that ill bit croft that sloped to the sea. When there wasn't a mist on the cold, stone parks there was more than likely the wheep of the rain, wheeling and dripping in from the sea that soughed and plashed by the land's stiff edge. Kinneff lay north, and at night in the south, if the sky was clear on the gloaming's edge, you'd see in that sky the Bervie lights come suddenly lit, far and away, with the quiet about you as you stood and looked, nothing to hear but a sea-bird's cry.

But feint the much time to look or to listen had Margaret Menzies of Tocherty toun. Day blinked and Meg did the same and was out, up out of her bed and about the house, making the porridge and rousting the bairns, and out to the byre to milk the three kye, the morning growing out in the east and a wind like a hail of knives from the hills. Syne back to the kitchen again she would be, and catch Jock, her eldest, a clour in the lug that he hadn't roused up his sisters and brothers; and rouse them herself, and feed them and scold, pull up their breeks and straighten their frocks and polish their shoes and set their caps straight. *Off you get and see you're not late,* she would cry, *and see you behave yourselves at the school. And tell the Dominie I'll be down the night to ask him what the mischief he meant by leathering Jeannie and her not well.*

They'd cry, *Ay, mother,* and go trotting away, a fair flock of the creatures, their faces red-scoured. Her own as red, like a meikle roan mare's, Meg'd turn at the door and go prancing in; and then at last, by the closet-bed, lean over and shake her man half-awake. *Come on, then, Willie, it's time you were up.*

And he'd groan and say *Is't?* and crawl out at last, a little bit thing like a weasel, Will Menzies, though some said that weasels were decent beside him. He was drinking himself into the grave, folk said, as coarse a little brute as you'd meet, bone-lazy forbye, and as sly as sin. Rampageous and ill with her tongue though she was, you couldn't but pity a woman like Meg tied up for life to a thing like *that.* But she'd more than a soft side still to the creature, she'd half-skelp the backside from any of the bairns she found in the telling of a small bit lie; but when Menzies would come paiching in of a noon and groan that he fair was tashed with his work, he'd mended all the ley fence that day and he doubted he'd need to be off to his bed – when he'd told her that and had ta'en to the blankets, and maybe in less than the space of an hour she'd hold out for the kye and see that he'd lied, the fence neither mended nor letten a-be, she'd just purse up her meikle wide mouth and say nothing, her eyes with a glint as though she half-laughed. And when he came drunken home from a mart she'd shoo the children out of the room, and take off his clothes and put him to bed, with an extra nip to keep off a chill.

She did half his work in the Tocherty parks, she'd yoke up the horse and the sholtie together, and kilt up her skirts till you'd see her great legs, and cry *Wissh!* like a man and turn a fair drill, the sea-gulls cawing in a cloud behind, the wind in her hair and the sea beyond. And Menzies with his sly-like eyes would be off on some drunken ploy to Kinneff or Stonehive. Man, you couldn't but think as you saw that steer it was well that there was a thing like marriage, folk held together and couldn't get apart; else a black look-out it well would be for the fusionless creature of Tocherty toun.

Well, he drank himself to his grave at last, less smell on the earth if maybe more in it. But she broke down and wept, it was awful to see, Meg Menzies weeping like a stricken horse, her eyes on the dead, quiet face of her man. And she ran from the house, she was gone all that night, though the bairns cried and cried her name up and down the parks in the sound of the sea. But next morning they found her back in their midst, brisk as ever, like a great-boned mare, ordering here and directing there, and a fine feed set the next day for the folk that came to the funeral of her orra man.

She'd four of the bairns at home when he died, the rest were in kitchen-service or fee'd, she'd seen to the settling of the queans herself; and twice when two of them had come home, complaining-like of their mistresses' ways, she'd thrashen the queans and taken them back – near scared the life from the doctor's wife, her that was mistress to young Jean Menzies. *I've skelped the lassie and brought you her back. But don't you ill-use her, or I'll skelp you as well.*

There was fair a speak about that at the time, Meg Menzies and the vulgar words she had used, folk told that she'd even said what was the place where she'd skelp the bit doctor's wife. And faith! that fair must have been a sore shock, the doctor's wife that was that genteel she'd never believed she'd a place like that.

Be that as it might, her man new dead, Meg wouldn't hear of leaving his toun. It was harvest then and she drove the reaper, up and down the long, clanging clay rings by the sea, she'd jump down smart at the head of a bout and go gathering and binding

3

swift as the wind, syne wheel in the horse to the cutting again. She led the stooks with her bairns to help, you'd see them at night, a drowsing cluster, under the moon on the harvesting cart.

And through that year and into the next and so till the speak died down in the Howe Meg Menzies worked the Tocherty toun; and faith, her crops came none so ill. She rode to the mart at Stonehive when she must, on the old box-cart, the old horse in the shafts, the cart behind with a sheep for sale or a birn of old hens that had finished with laying. And a butcher once tried to make a bit joke, *That's a sheep like yourself, fell long in the tooth.* And Meg answered up, neighing like a horse, and all heard: *Faith, then, if you've got a spite against teeth I've a clucking hen in the cart outbye. It's as toothless and senseless as you are, near.*

Then word got about of her eldest son, Jock Menzies that was fee'd up Allardyce way. The creature of a loon had had fair a conceit since he'd won a prize at a ploughing match – not for his ploughing, but for his good looks; and the queans about were as daft as himself, he'd only to nod and they came to his heel; and the stories told they came further than that. Well, Meg'd heard the stories and paid no heed, till the last one came, she was fell quick then.

Soon's she heard it she hove out the old bit bike that her daughter Kathie had bought for herself, and got on the thing and went cycling away, down through the Bervie braes in that Spring, the sun was out and the land lay green, with a blink of mist that was blue on the hills, as she came to the toun where Jock was fee'd she saw him out in a park by the road, ploughing, the black loam smooth like a ribbon turning and wheeling at the tail of the plough. Another billy came ploughing behind, Meg Menzies watched till they reached the rig-end, her great chest heaving like a meikle roan's, her eyes on the shape of the furrows they made. And they drew to the end and drew the horse out, and Jock cried *Ay*, and she answered back *Ay*, and looked at the drill, and gave a bit snort, *If your looks win prizes, your ploughing never will.*

4

Jock laughed. *Fegs, then, I'll not greet for that,* and chirked to his horses and turned them about. But she cried him *Just bide you a minute, my lad. What's this that I hear about you and Ag Grant?*

He drew up short then, and turned right red, the other childe as well, and they both gave a laugh, as plough-childes do when you mention a quean they've known over-well in more ways than one. And Meg snapped *It's an answer I want, not a cockerel's cackle: I can hear that at home on my own dunghill. What are you to do about Ag and her pleiter?*

And Jock said *Nothing,* impudent as you like, and next minute Meg was in over the dyke and had hold of his lug and shook him and it till the other childe ran and caught at her nieve. *Faith, mistress, you'll have his lug off!* he cried. But Meg Menzies turned like a mare on new grass, *Keep off or I'll have yours as well!*

So he kept off and watched, fair a story he'd to tell when he rode out that night to go courting his quean. For Meg held to the lug till it near came off and Jock swore that he'd put things right with Ag Grant. She let go the lug then and looked at him grim: *See that you do and get married right quick, you're the like that need loaded with a birn of bairns – to keep you out of the jail, I jaloose. It needs smeddum to be either right coarse or right kind.*

They were wed before the month was well out, Meg found them a cottar house to settle, and gave them a bed and a press she had, and two-three more sticks from Tocherty toun. And she herself led the wedding dance, the minister in her arms, a small bit childe; and 'twas then as she whirled him about the room, he looked like a rat in the teeth of a tyke, that he thanked her for seeing Ag out of her soss, *There's nothing like a marriage for redding things up.* And Meg Menzies said *Eh?* and then she said *Ay,* but queer-like, he supposed she'd no thought on the thing. Syne she slipped off to sprinkle thorns in the bed, and to hang below it the great hand-bell that the bothy-billies took them to every bit marriage.

Well, that was Jock married and at last off her hands. But she'd plenty left still, Dod, Kathleen and Jim that were still

5

at the school, Kathie a limner that alone tongued her mother, Jeannie that next led trouble to her door. She'd been found at her place, the doctor's it was, stealing some money and they sent her home. Syne news of the thing got into Stonehive, the police came out and tormented her sore, she swore she never had stolen a meck, and Meg swore with her, she was black with rage. And folk laughed right hearty, fegs! that was a clour for meikle Meg Menzies, her daughter a thief!

But it didn't last long, it was only three days when folk saw the doctor drive up in his car. And out he jumped and went striding in through the close and met face to face with Meg at the door. And he cried *Well, mistress, I've come over for Jeannie.* and she glared at him over her high, skeugh nose, *Ay, have you so then? And why, may I speir?*

So he told her why, the money they'd missed had been found at last, in a press by the door; somebody or other had left it there, thoughtless, when paying a grocer or such at the door. And Jeannie – he'd come over to take Jean back.

But Meg glared *Ay, well, you've made another mistake. Out of this you and your thieving suspicions together!* The doctor turned red, *You're making a miserable error* – and Meg said *I'll make you mince-meat in a minute.*

So he didn't wait that, she didn't watch him go, but went ben to the kitchen where Jeannie was sitting, her face chalkwhite as she'd heard them speak. And what happened then a story went round, Jim carried it to school, and it soon spread out. Meg sank in a chair, they thought she was greeting; syne she raised up her head and they saw she was laughing, near as fearsome the one as the other, they thought. *Have you any cigarettes?* she snapped sudden at Jean, and Jean quavered *No,* and Meg glowered at her cold. *Don't sit there and lie. Gang bring them to me.* And Jean brought them, her mother took the pack in her hand. *Give's hold of a match till I light up the thing. Maybe smoke'll do good for the crow that I got in the throat last night by the doctor's house.*

Well, in less than a month she'd got rid of Jean – packed off

to Brechin the quean was and soon, got married to a creature
that worked down there – some clerk that would have left her
sore in the lurch but that Meg went down to the place on her
bike, and there, so the story went, kicked the childe so that he
couldn't sit down for a fortnight, near. No doubt that was just
a bit lie that they told, but faith! Meg Menzies had herself to
blame, the reputation she'd gotten in the Howe, folk said *She'll
meet with a sore heart yet.* But devil a sore was there to be seen,
Jeannie was married and was fair genteel.

Kathleen was next to leave home at the term. She was tall,
like Meg, and with red hair as well, but a thin, fine face, long
eyes blue-grey like the hills on a hot day, and a mouth with
lips you thought over thick. And she cried *Ah well, I'm off then,
mother.* And Meg cried *See you behave yourself.* And Kathleen
cried *Maybe; I'm not at school now.*

Meg stood and stared after the slip of a quean, you'd have
thought her half-angry, half near to laughing, as she watched
that figure, so slender and trig, with its shoulders square-set,
slide down the hill on the wheeling bike, swallows were dipping
and flying by Kinneff, she looked light and free as a swallow
herself, the quean as she biked away from her home, she turned
at the bend and waved and whistled, she whistled like a loon
and as loud, did Kath.

Jim was the next to leave from the school, he bided at home
and he took no fee, a quiet-like loon, and he worked the toun,
and, wonder of wonders, Meg took a rest. Folk said that age
was telling a bit on even Meg Menzies at last. The grocer made
hints at that one night, and Meg answered up smart as ever
of old. *Damn the age! But I've finished the trauchle of the bairns at
last, the most of them married or still over young. I'm as swack as
ever I was, my lad. But I've just got the notion to be a bit sweir.*

Well, she'd hardly begun on that notion when faith! ill the
news that came up to the place from Seggest. Kathleen, her
quean that was fee'd down there, she'd ta'en up with some
coarse old childe in a bank, he'd left his wife, they were off
together, and she but a bare sixteen years old.

And that proved the truth of what folk were saying, Meg Menzies she hardly paid heed to the news, just gave a bit laugh like a neighing horse and went on with the work of park and byre, cool as you please – ay, getting fell old.

No more was heard of the quean or the man till a two years or more had passed and then word came up to the Tocherty someone had seen Kath Menzies at last – and where do you think? Out on a boat that was coming from Australia. She was working as stewardess on that bit boat, and the childe that saw her was young John Robb, an emigrant back from his uncle's farm, near starved to death he had been down there. She hadn't met in with him near till the end, the boat close to Southampton the evening they met. And she'd known him at once, though he not her, she'd cried *John Robb!* and he'd answered back *Ay?* and looked at her canny in case it might be the creature was looking for a tip from him. Syne she'd laughed, *Don't you know me, then, you gowk? I'm Kathie Menzies you knew long syne – I ran off with the banker from Segget!*

He was clean dumbfoundered, young Robb, and he gaped, and then they shook hands and she spoke some more, though she hadn't much time, they were serving up dinner for the first-class folk, aye dirt that are ready to eat and to drink. *If ever you get near to Tocherty toun, tell Meg I'll get home and see her some time. Ta-ta!* And then she was off with a smile, young Robb he stood and he stared where she'd been, he thought her the bonniest thing that he'd seen all the weary weeks that he'd been from home.

And this was the tale that he brought to Tocherty, Meg sat and listened and smoked like a tink, forbye herself there was young Jim there, and Jock and his wife and their three bit bairns, he'd fair changed with marriage, had young Jock Menzies. For no sooner had he taken Ag Grant to his bed than he'd started to save, grown mean as dirt, in a three-four years he'd finished with feeing, now he rented a fell big farm for himself, well-stocked it was, and he fee'd two men. Jock himself had grown thin and mean in a way, like his father but worse,

8

his bothy childes said, old Menzies at least could take a bit dram and get lost to the world but the son was that mean he might drink rat-poison and take no harm, 'twould feel at home in a stomach like his.

Well, that was Jock and he sat and heard the story of Kath and her say on the boat. *Ay, still a coarse bitch, I have not a doubt. Well, if she never comes back to the Mearns, in Segget you cannot but redden with shame when a body will ask 'Was Kath Menzies your sister?'*

And Ag, she'd grown a great sumph of a woman, she nodded to that, it was only too true, a sore thing it was on decent bit folk that they should have any relations like Kath.

But Meg just sat there and smoked, and said never a word, as though she thought nothing heard worth a yea or a nay. Young Robb had ta'en fair a fancy to Kath, and he near boiled up when he heard Jock speak, him and the wife that he'd married from her shame. So he left them short, and went raging home, and wished for one that Kath would come back, a Summer noon as he cycled home, snipe were calling in the Auchindreich moor where the cattle stood with their tails a-switch, the Grampians rising far and behind, Kinraddie spread like a map for show, its ledges veiled in a mist from the sun. You felt on that day a wild, daft unease, man, beast and bird: as though something were missing and lost from the world, and Kath was the thing that John Robb missed, she'd something in her that minded a man of a house that was builded upon a hill.

Folk thought that that was maybe the last they would ever hear of young Kath Menzies and her ill-getted ways. So fair stammy-gastered they were with the news she'd come back to Mearns, she was down in Stonehive, in a grocer's shop there, as calm as could be, selling out tea and cheese and such-like with no blush of shame on her face at all, to decent women that were properly wed, and had never looked on men but their own, and only on them with their galluses tied.

It just showed you the way that the world was going to

allow an ill quean like that in a shop, some folk protested to the creature that owned it, but he just shook his head, *Ah well, she works fine; and what else she does is no business of mine.* So you well might guess there was more than business between the man and Kath Menzies.

And Meg heard the news and went into Stonehive, driving her sholtie, and stopped at the shop. And some in the shop knew who she was, and minded the things she had done long syne to other bit bairns of hers that went wrong; and they waited with their breaths held up with delight. But all that Meg did was to nod to Kath, *Ay, well, then, it's you. . . . Ay, mother, just that. . . . Two pounds of syrup and see that it's good.*

And not another word passed between them, Meg Menzies that once would have ta'en such a quean and skelped her to rights before you could wink. Going home from Stonehive she stopped by the farm where young Robb was fee'd, he was out in the hayfield coling the hay, and she nodded to him, grim, with her high horse face. *What's this that I hear about you and Kath Menzies?*

He turned right red, but he wasn't ashamed. *I've no idea — though I hope it's the worst. . . . It fell near is. . . . Then I wish it was true, she might marry me, then, as I've prigged her to do.*

Oh, have you so, then? said Meg, and drove home, as though the whole matter was a nothing to her.

But next Tuesday the postman brought a bit note, from Kathie it was to her mother at Tocherty. *Dear mother, John Robb's going out to Canada, and wants me to marry him and go with him there. I've told him instead I'll go with him and see what he's like as a man — and then marry him at leisure, if I feel in the mood. But he's hardly any money, and we want to borrow some, so he and I are coming over on Sunday. I hope that you'll have dumpling for tea. Your own daughter, Kath.*

Well, Meg passed that letter over to Jim, he glowered at it dour, *I know — near all the Howe's heard. What are you going to do, now, mother?*

But Meg just lighted a cigarette and said nothing, she'd

smoked like a tink since that steer with Jean. There was promise
of strange on-goings at Tocherty by the time that the Sabbath
day was come. For Jock came there on a visit as well, him and
his wife, and besides him was Jeannie, her that had married
the clerk down in Brechin, and she brought the bit creature,
he fair was a toff; and he stepped like a cat through the sharn
in the close; and when he had heard the story of Kath, her and
her plan and John Robb and all, he was shocked near to death,
and so was his wife. And Jock Menzies gaped and gave a mean
laugh. *Ay, coarse to the bone, ill-getted I'd say if it wasn't that we
came of the same bit stock. Ah well, she'll fair have to tramp to Canada,
eh mother? – if she's looking for money from you.*

And Meg answered quiet, *No, I wouldn't say that. I've the
money all ready for them when they come.*

You could hear the sea plashing down soft on the rocks,
there was such a dead silence in Tocherty house. And then
Jock habbered like a cock with fits, *What, give silver to one who
does as she likes, and won't marry as you made the rest of us marry?
Give silver to one who's no more than a –*

And he called his sister an ill name enough, and Meg sat
and smoked, looking over the parks. *Ay, just that. You see, she
takes after myself.*

And Jeannie squeaked *How?* and Meg answered her sudden,
a neigh that fair shook the bit walls of the room, *She's fit to be
free and to make her own choice, the same as myself and the same kind
of choice. There was none of the rest of you fit to do that, you'd to marry
or burn, so I married you quick. But Kath and me could afford to find
out. It all depends if you've smeddum or not.*

She stood up then and put her cigarette out, and looked at
the gaping gowks she had mothered. *I never married your father,
you see. I could never make up my mind about Will. But maybe our
Kath will find something surer. Here's her and her man coming up the
road.*

GREENDEN

Folk laughed when they heard of the creatures coming to sit them down in the farm of Greenden, that lay west of the Tulloch by Bervie Water. It was a forty-fifty acre place, the Den, wet in the bottom, as well it might be, so low it lay there in its woods. In the midst stood the biggings; they were old and right dark: from the kitchen door you looked round and up at a jungle, near, you would say, lost from the world, so close around and between the trees the broom plants grew, and the whins. But when night came, sometimes over the trees and the rank, wild waste of the moor, you'd see through a narrow pass in the woods the last of the sun as it kindled a light on the Grampain Hills and went off to its bed. And that light in the mirk was near as much as a man would see of the world outby from the kitchen door of Greenden.

Well, old Grant had farmed there till he died, a steady old stock — fair strong in the hands if weak in the head, was the speak of Murdoch of Mains. For a body hardly ever made out what he said; he would whisper and whisper, whispering even as he girned at his horse in the lithe of the woods that watched Greenden. Soon's he'd been ta'en, the old mistress moved her into Drumlithie and took a bit cottage, and lived on his silver; and sometimes she'd say to a crony at night: 'It's fine to be here and with sonsy folk.' They thought at first she would miss her man; the minister came, the Free Kirk loon, he snuffled right godly and said through his nose: 'You'll meet him Above, Mistress Grant.' But at that she gave a kind of a start, near dropped the teapot, she did, when he spoke. 'Will I, then? Ay, fegs, I'll confess that I hadn't reckoned that.'

Well, that was the Grants gone out of Greenden. There the ill place lay as the winter wore on not an offer the factor had for it either; a man could sweat out his guts on a better ploy than manuring the dour red clay of the Den. Syne the news went round it was let at last: the factor had let it to no farming body, but a creature from the town, from Glasgow it was; he'd never handled a plough or a graip before, and Murdoch at the Mains had a story about him. For he'd driven the creature and his wife round the district, and as they went by the parks at Pittendreich they'd seen a roller of old Pittendreich's there, out in the ley the thing was lying. And the body of a woman had gleyed at the thing: 'What a shame to let it get rusty, isn't it?' and looked at Murdoch like a fool of a bairn.

Folk took that through hand with a laugh here and there; some said it was surely a lie, though gey witty, for everybody knew that the Murdoch brute could lie like a tink when the mood was on him, fell often that was. True or not, you began to think of the creatures – Simpson the name was – that had taken Greenden and were moving in there at the February end. Ay, they'd find it a change from their Glasgow streets; they didn't know what it was to work, the dirt that came from the towns.

Well, come at last the Simpsons did to Greenden; their gear and furniture came by Bervie, and the Simpson man went there to hire two carts for the carting down of the stuff. Webster the grocer had no rounds that day, and he hired out his carts and drove one himself, George Simpson the other. It was late at night when they came to the Den, down through the thick woods, larch it was there, so close the trunks that the night was dark though the light shone still out on the high road that walked by the sea. But they saw in the Den as they wound down there a lantern kindled at last in the mirk, kindled and shining from the kitchen door. And when the carts came rumbling into the close there the wife of Simpson was standing and waiting, the lantern held in her hand.

And Webster took a bit keek at the creature, and half thought she must be but Simpson's daughter, no wife she looked; she was thin and slim, bonny in a way, and her eyes were kind.

She laughed up at Simpson coming behind, syne smiled at the grocer, and cried up in an English-like voice: 'You've been long; I thought I'd have to spend the night down here – all alone by myself in Greenden.'

Alec Webster said: 'Well, mistress, you'd have ta'en no ill.' And she nodded to that: 'I know that fine. . . . And, of course, the country's lovely to live in.' And she smiled at him like a daft-like quean. He glowered back at her; canny, slow and quiet Alec, he couldn't make head nor tail of her yet, her laugh and that quiver she hid in her laugh.

Syne he loosed and helped them in with their gear, a great clutter of stuff they'd brought up from Glasgow. George Simpson he puffed and paiched right sore, big though he was, with a sappy big face, and a look on that face as though some childe had ta'en him a hard kick in the backside. But his lungs were gey bad, he told to the grocer; he'd come out to the country for his lungs, he said. And when Murdoch at Mains heard of that speak he said: 'Faith, the creature's more like to mislay his anatomy than pick up a bit on the ill clay rigs of the Den.'

So there were the two of them settled in there, Simpson and the little bit snippet of a wife: she looked light enough for a puff of wind to blow her from her kitchen door at night when she opened that door to come out to the grocer as he drove his van down for her orders on Friday. Alec Webster was a kindly stock, and he cried: 'Losh, Mistress, you're not in your Glasgow now, you'll fair need to keep yourself wrapped up.' But she only laughed: 'I'm fine – oh, listen to the trees!' And the grocer listened, and heard them sough, and turned him his head and glowered at the woods: they were just as aye they had been, he thought; why should a man stand still and listen? He asked her, Ellen Simpson, that, and keeked at her white, still stare. And she started again, and smiled at him, queer. 'Oh, nothing. Sorry. But I can't but listen.'

Well, maybe she knew what she meant; he didn't. He sold her her orders – she fair had a lot – and drove away up the February dark; and as he was driving he heard in the dark a

hoasting and hacking out there by the barn, and he thought
of the Simpson childe and his lungs. Faith, he'd come to the
wrong place here for his lungs; it wasn't long likely he would
store the kiln.

Mistress Murdoch went down to tea at Greenden. But she
couldn't abide George Simpson's mistress, the creature fair
got on to her nerves with her flitting here and her tripping
there, and her laugh, and the meikle eyes of her in the small doll
face that she had. She said it was Simpson she pitied, poor man,
with lungs like his and a wife like that, little comfort by day
and less in his bed; she herself would rather sleep with a fluff
of a feather than depend on *that* on a coldrife night.

And then, as daft-like a blether as ever you heard, the story
got about how it was that they'd come to move up from Glasgow
to Greenden toun. George Simpson himself it was that told
it, one night he dropped in at the Murdoch house – he would
go a bit walk there now and again and gley at the daughter,
Jeannie. And the way of their moving from Glasgow had been
when his lungs took bad it was plain that he wouldn't last out
a long while at his clerking work; he was fair for the knackers'
yard, you would say. The doctors said he should leave the town,
but he'd little fancy for that himself, and his wife had less: she
was town-bred, and feared at the country, Ellen; or so he'd aye
thought. For next Sunday he'd gone with her to their kirk,
and then it was that a hymn was sung, and it fair seemed to
change Ellen Simpson's mind. And the hymn was the one that
begins with the words:

> *There is a green hill far away,*
>   *Beyond a city wall,*
> *Where the dear Lord was crucified,*
>   *Who died to save us all.*

So when the Simpsons got back to their house Ellen Simpson
had kept whispering and remembering that tune, and sudden-
like she said they must leave the town; they must find a farm
where George could work in the open and mend his ill lungs.

Well, he'd hardly hear of the thing at first, as he told to
the Murdochs that night at their house; he thought that work
on a farm would kill him. But Ellen had set her mind on the
plan, so he set about looking for a place to please her. He'd but
little silver to stock up a steading, and land in the south was
far over dear, but up in the Mearns he came on Greenden, its
rent just inside the reach of his pouch. So he'd ta'en his wife
up to see it; she'd stared, down in the hollow, and seemed half
ta'en aback. And then she'd said they must take it, and take it
they did, and here now they were; and *she* liked it fine.

And fine well she might do, the coarse creature, folk said.
It wasn't her had to face up the rains of that year, or the coarse
ploughing of the ill red clay of Greenden. Ay, Simpson was a
fine bit childe, a bit dour, but faith! he was surely fair a fool
as well to let himself be ta'en from a fine town job out to the
pleiter and soss of a farm, to pleasure that creature his wife and
the fancies she'd got from hearing a hymn in a kirk. Folk with
sense knew fine that hymns were just things that you sang at,
douce, and then you forgot.

Wet it was that spring: March came flooding in rains down
the length and breadth of the guttering Howe; every night
you'd hear the swash of the water if your place in the bed was
next to the wall; the gulls were up from the Bervie beaches
and cawing at all hours over the parks. Down in Greenden it
was worse than most, and Simpson with his hoast, poor childe,
might well have kept in his bed and blankets, but his creature
of a wife wouldn't hear of that, laughing at him, affronting him
into a rage. 'Come on, now, George, the day's half dead! And
it's fine, a good day for the plough.'

So out he'd to get, and out with his pair, and go slow-stepping
up and down the ley haughs that lined the deep Den. His
ploughing was fair a sight for sore eyes; of a Sunday the bothy
billies would come over, they'd take a bit dander down to the
Den and stand and laugh as they looked at the drills, they went
this way and that: 'Dam't, man, they've but little sense in the
towns!' Syne they'd hear Mistress Simpson crying to her hens,

and see her, small, like a snippet of a doll, flit over the close on some errand or another. The poor Simpson childe kept to his bed on the Sundays.

Well, the spring wore on, fine planting weather came, by May the sun was a blaze of heat; up and down the long Howe folk shook their heads. With a spring like this you might well depend that you'd have a summer with sleet, most-like. But it was well enough while it went, and Murdoch of Mains took a dander down to the Den now and then to see how the Simpson man was fairing. And, faith! he'd been kept with his nose at the grind; he'd his parks as well forward as any other place. Murdoch hadn't set eyes on him near for a month, and fair got a shock as he stopped his roller and stood by to speak. He'd grown thicker and bigger, his face filled out; you could hardly see the town in him at all. And Murdoch said: 'Ay, man, you're fair a bit farmer!'

And Simpson smiled wan, right patient-like though, with his sappy red face like an ill-used nout's, and said: 'Maybe,' and paiched to listen at his lungs. And then he told that each night he went to his bed with a back like to break, but Ellen just laughed. She didn't know what an illness was; he wasn't the man to fear her and tell her the truth. So Murdoch saw fine how the thing was going, the Simpson childe working himself to his grave, with his coarse lungs, too, to please his coarse wife. There was nothing he could do in the matter, he thought, but he said they'd aye be pleased to see Simpson at Mains. He said nothing of Ellen, the bit wife, in that; there was damn the pleasure to be had in the creature; with her laugh and her listening and the flutter of her eyes, she fairly got on a body's bit nerves.

What with rain and with heat the Den was green-lush right early that year – the grocer thought it came thicker than ever he minded – the broom stopped up the aisles of the larch that stretched up the braes from the old brown biggings of the Den. Ellen Simpson would come running out to the door as she heard the sound of his wheels on the close, and cry him good-day, and bring him the eggs, and stand still while he counted, a slow, canny childe; but once he raised up his head and said: 'Losh, but it's still!'

And the two of them stood there and listened in that quiet, not a sound to be heard or a thing to be seen beyond the green cup that stood listening around. And Ellen Simpson smiled white and said: 'Yes, it is still – and I'll take two loaves and some tea now, please.'

And Webster took a look at her: thinner she'd grown, more a wisp than ever, but still with her smile, and he liked her fine, near the only soul in the district that did. Most said she'd grown thinner with temper, faith! girning at her man to get out and start work, and him no more than an invalid, like.

Just luck she hadn't his death on her hands, and you couldn't blame him that he fell in the habit, nearly every bit evening he would do it now, of taiking away over the brae from the Den to the Mains and the Murdochs; they liked him fine. Jeannie Murdoch and he would flirt and would fleer – no harm in their fun, folk 'greed about that: the poor stock was no doubt in need of a laugh, him and that wife with her flutterings that fair set your hackles on edge. He was better than he'd been, he'd confess, would Simpson; all the more reason why he wanted some cheer when he came in about to his own fire at night, not aye to be listening to somebody cry: 'Oh, George, do you think your lungs are near better?'

And Jeannie Murdoch would say: 'No, I'm sure. Sit you down. I'll make you a fine cup of tea.' And George Simpson would laugh out his big, sappy laugh: 'Faith! you're fine as you're bonny, Jean, lass.'

And Murdoch and his mistress would hear them and gley, Mistress Murdoch pull down her meikle bit face; maybe she thought Jeannie went over far with a man that was married – no more than fun though their speak might be. If it wasn't for that snippet of a creature, Ellen, you'd think Simpson as fine a goodson as you'd meet; a bit slow at the uptake, maybe a bit dour, but a pretty, upstanding childe he was now.

Folk wondered a bit what she thought of those jaunts, Ellen Simpson down by her lone in Greenden. But she never said a word to a soul about them, not that she saw a many to speak to; she'd just smile, and go running and bring you some tea, kind enough you supposed that the creature was, but you'd never get yourself to like her, you'd know; she'd set you all unease till you'd sit and wonder what ailed yourself – till going up home through the dark you'd be filled with fancies daft as a carrying woman, as though the trees moved and the broom was whispering, and some beast with quiet breath came padding in your tracks; and you'd look, and 'twas only a whin that you'd passed. And you'd heave a great breath, outside of the Den, up in the light of the evening sun, though the Den below was already in shadow.

But of nights as that summer wore on to its close she took to standing at her kitchen door, while the light drew in and the dark came close: now and then some soul would come on her there, near startle her out of her skin as he cried: 'Ay, mistress, it's a fine bit night.' And she'd laugh, with her hand at her breast, daft-like, and then turn her head as though half she'd forgotten you and look up and away out over the trees, and you'd look the same way and see feint the thing. And then maybe you'd look harder and see what it was; it was from the kitchen door along of Greenden that the swathe of the trees and the broom was broken, and through the hollow that was left in the gloaming the sun struck light on the Grampian slopes, long miles away and across the Mearns, shining immediate, yet distant and blue, their green earth-hazed in the heather-bells. And that was the thing that she stood and watched, as a daftie would, and you'd scrape your feet, and you'd give a bit hoast, and she'd start and switch round, her face gone white, and say: 'Oh, I'm sorry, I'd forgotten you were here. Was it George that you wanted to see?'

Well, that was in June, and the June-end came, as bonny as ever it came in the Howe; folk meeting the Simpson man on the road would cry to him for a joke. 'Ay, man, you're fair smothered away from the world in Greenden.' And, faith! they spoke but the truth, so high was the broom with a mantling of bloom, and the trees were a wall fair blinding the place. George Simpson made out of it every bit night, over to the Mains' new barn they were building; he'd pretend it was the barn he went over to see, but he'd edge away from it soon as he might, taik round to the kitchen, and Jeannie would blush and cry: 'Step away in, Mr Simpson. How are you? I'm sure you are tired.'

Well, that barn it was, Webster was to swear, brought things to an end to that steer at Greenden. He never told the story in a neighbour-like way, he never did that, and he wasn't much liked, for he'd never much news to give to a body when you spoke to him at the tail of his van and would drop a bit hint that you'd like to know why the Gordon quean was getting gey stout, and if Wallace was as coarse as they said to his wife, and such newsy-like bits of an interest to folk. He'd just grunt when you spoke and start counting the eggs, and say he was damned if he knew or he cared. So he told the Greenden tale to none but his wife; he thought her the same as himself, did Alec. But faith! she could claik a tink from a door, and soon it was known up and down the Howe, every bit of the happening that night at Greenden.

For he'd driven down there late, as aye he had done, the grocer, and was coming in by the yard, when he met Ellen Simpson come running up the road; her face was white in the fading light, and twice as she ran he saw her fall; and she picked herself up with blood on her face where a stone had cut as she fell. And Webster stopped his horse and jumped off the van and went running to meet her, and he cried: 'God, mistress, what's ta'en you – what's wrong?'

And she gabbled as he held her, he saw her eyes wild, syne she quieted a minute and covered her eyes, and shivered, hot though the June night was. Then she whispered sudden, he shivered himself: 'They've done something to my hill, they have taken it away! Oh, I can't stand it now, I can't, I can't!'

And Webster said: 'What?' He was clean dumbfoundered; and he thought in a flash of old Grant of Greenden – he also had whispered and whispered like that. But she pointed up across the larch-hill and the broom, and he gowked, did the grocer, and saw nothing for a while. Syne he saw that there rose through that howe in the woods, through which you'd once see the light gleam on the hills, the roof and the girders of Murdoch's new barn. He stared at the thing, and then stared at the woman, and at that she broke down and cried like a bairn; she'd no shame before him, she was surely daft.

'Oh, I can't stand it longer in this hateful place! It's smothering and killing me, down and lost here, I've been frightened, so frightened, since the first hour here. I've tried not to show it, and I *know* that it's nothing, but the trees – they hate me, the fields, and at night. . . . Oh, I can't stand it longer, not even for George, now they've blocked up that sight of the hill that was mine!'

And she cried out more of that stite, and the grocer – he'd aye liked her – was fair in a way. 'Whisht, mistress, go in and lie down,' he said, but she whispered: 'Don't leave me, don't leave me, I'm frightened!' And the dark came then down over the broom, and the horse stood champing and scraping its hooves, and a howlet began to hoot in the larch while Webster sat by her in the kitchen to quiet her. And she whispered once: 'George – he's safe now, he's safe, God died, but I needn't, He saved him, not I.' And what she meant by that Alec neither knew nor could guess, and syne she was whispering again in her terror: 'The trees and the broom, keep off the trees; it's growing so dark I can't see it, the green hill. . . .'

But at last she grew quiet; he told her to lie down. She went ben from the kitchen, and he stood and thought. And he minded her man might be at the Mains; he went out and drew round his grocer's van, and got into it and drove up out of the Den, and whipped his bit beast to a trot as he drew nigh the Mains.

And folk told that when he got there he went stamping in the kitchen: George Simpson was sitting with Jeannie and her father; the mistress was off to the pictures at Bervie. And Alec Webster cried: 'Leave your courting until you're a widower; have you no shame at all to abandon your wife night after night in that hell of a Den?' And George Simpson stood up and blustered: 'You mucker——', and the grocer said: 'Away, raise your hand up to me, you big, well-fed bullock, and I'll crack your jaw where you stand.' Old Murdoch came in between them then, and he cried: 'What is't? What's wrong?'

So Webster told Simpson his wife was gey queer; was he or was he not going home? And Simpson scowled and said: 'Yes,' and went out with the grocer, and that childe swung round his weary bit horse and lashed it to a trot, and out into the road, and so, in their time, by the track to the Den. And there it was dark as a fireless lum, but far off as they neared to the biggings they heard a voice singing – singing so strange that it raised their hair:

There is a green hill far away,
  Beyond a city wall,
Where the dear Lord was crucified,
  Who died to save us all——

And it suddenly ceased, and Webster swore, and he lashed the horse, and they came to the close, and Webster jumped down and ran into the house. Behind him went Simpson, more slow – he was feared. In the kitchen it was dark and still as they came. Then the grocer slipped, there was something slippery and wet on the floor. So he kindled a match, and they both looked up, and they saw what it was, and it turned them sick. And a waft of wind came in from the door, and the Shape from the beam swung to and fro.

And Webster turned round and went blundering out, as

though he couldn't see, and he called to Simpson: 'Take her down and I'll go for the doctor, man.'

But he knew right well that that would help nothing, and the thought went with him as he drove through the woods, up out of the Den, to the road that walked by the sea, and the green hills that stood to peer with quiet faces in the blow of the wind from the sunset's place.

SIM

What profit hath a man of all his labour which he taketh under the sun? – Ecclesiastes i., 4.

Sim Wilson came of a fell queer stock, his mother a spinner at the Segget Mills, his father a soldier killed by the Boers. When news of that killing came up to Segget the wife just laughed – 'Worse folk than the Boers' – and went on with the tink-like life that she led. In time that fair grew a scandal in Segget, a body wasn't safe to let her man out of her sight for a minute, in case he met in with that Wilson creature, and was led all agley with her coarse green glower.

Sim was no more than five years old when at last things came to a head in Segget, his mother went off on a moonflight flit with the widow Grant's son and half of her silver. Folks wondered which of the two would last longest. Young Sim was left in an emptied house, till his auntie that bade in a house by Drumlithie took pity on the loon and had him down there. She came all a-fuss and a-pant with pity, the aunty, a meikle big creash of a woman, and she said to Sim, 'You're my dawtie now.' And Sim said, 'Maybe – if you'll leave me a-be.'

Faith, that was his only care from the first, as sweir a nickum as you'd meet, folk said, sweir at the school as he was at his home, it was a fair disease with the ill-getted loon. And an impudent creature he was, forbye, with his glinting black hair and his glinting green eyes, he'd truant from school more often than not and be off in the summer to sleep in the sun, under the lithe of a whin or a stook. And once, he was then about ten years old, his auntie came on him high on the brae, in the heat, his chin in his hands as he keeked down through the veils of broom at the teams, steaming at work

24

in the parks below. She cried, 'You coarse brute, why aren't you at school? Aren't you fair black affronted to lie there and stink?'

Well, Sim just sneered, not feered a wee bit, 'No, I'm not. I was watching those fools in that park. You won't find me sossing and chaving like that when I'm a man with a fee of my own. The dafties – not to take a bit rest! ... Lessons? Away, do you think I am soft?'

And he stuck out his tongue and slipped under her arm, his auntie near greeting with rage as he ran. But she couldn't catch up, loaded down with her creash. Sim was soon out of sight on his way up the hill. He spent the whole day lying flat on his back, the only sweir soul in the hash of the Howe.

Folk said that he'd come to an ill-like end, his sweirty would eat to his bones and they'd rot. But then, near the middle of his thirteenth year, he heard the news in his class at the school that the prize for dux that year was a pound; and all of a jiffy he started to work, like mad, near blinded himself of a night with reading and writing and learning his lessons, the hills hardly saw him except back of a book. And he'd cleverness in him, sweir though he'd been, he was dux for that year and the dominie delighted.

He said to the loon, 'You'll do even better,' but Sim just sneered in his impudent way, 'I'm finished with chaving at lessons and dirt. I've tried, and I know that they're not worth the sweat.' The dominie was fair took aback to hear that. 'You'll gang a hard gait through the world, I fear.' And Sim said, 'Maybe; but I'll gang it myself. And I'll know what I'm getting ere I gang it at all.'

He fee'd his first fee at Upperhill in Kinraddie. Big-boned he had grown, and supple and swack, but as sweir as ever and an ill-liked brute. He'd sneer at his elders and betters in the bothy, 'What, work my guts out for that red-headed rat? Whatever for, can you tell me that? Show me a thing that is worth my tràuchle, and I'll work you all off the face of the earth!'

The foreman there was a canny-like childe, and the only one that could bear with Sim. They both stayed on for a four-five years, Sim sweir as ever, with his glinting green eyes, he'd a bigger power for lazing around than a pig in a ree, was the speak of the bothy. And young and buirdly, well-happed like a hog, he'd doze through the work of the Upper-hill parks, goodnatured enough were he letten alone. But sometimes he'd stop from making his brose, of a night, when the bothy was lit by the fire, 'And to think that the morn we'll be doing the same!' The billies in the bothy would maybe say 'What?' and he'd say, 'Why, making more brose to eat! And the night after that and the night after that. And we'll get up the morn and slave and chave for that red-headed rat – and go to our beds and get up again. Whatever for, can you tell me that?'

And the brute, in one of those unco-like moods, would go off on a jaunting down to Segget; and take a dram or so in the Arms; and look round about for a spinner to spite. And if there were such Sim would swagger up to him, 'Ay, man, you've a look on your face I don't like. And I don't much like your face the look's on.' The spinner would maybe look Sim up and down, with a sneer, and call him a clod-hopping clown, and Sim would take him a bash in the face, and next minute the spinners would pile in on Sim; and when he got back to Upperhill bothy he'd look as though he'd been fed through the teeth of a mill. But he'd say as he got in his bed, 'That was fine. Man, I fairly stirred up that dirt down in Segget!' And next day he'd be sleepy and sweir as before.

Syne he met with Kate Duthie at a dance down in Segget, she was narrow and red-haired, with a pointed chin and hard grey eyes you could strike a spunk on, a quean that worked as maid at the Manse. Well, Sim took a look at her, she one at him; and he fair went daft that minute about her. He waited till that dance was over and said, 'Can I have the next?' and Kate Duthie said, 'Maybe. Who might you be?' And Sim Wilson told her, and Kate gave a laugh, 'Oh, only a ploughman.'

As the Upperhill lads walked back that night in a bunch from the dance they had been to in Segget, Sim told them the speak of the grey-eyed quean. The foreman said, 'And who might she think that she is? A joskin's as good as any damned maid.' Sim shook his head, 'Most, maybe; not her. Faith, man, but she's bonny, and I wish that I had her.'

Well, that was only the beginning of the stir, his sweirty went like a mist in June, he was out nearly every bit night after that, down at the Manse or hanging round Segget. Kate sometimes saw him and sometimes she didn't, she kept as cool as a clayed-up coulter. At last it came to a night Sim said, 'I'm thinking of marrying'; Kate Duthie said, 'Oh, well, I wish you joy.' And Sim said, 'Ay, I'll get that fine – if you'll come and provide it.'

Kate laughed in his face and told him plain she wasn't cut out for a ploughman's wife, to drag through her days in a cottar house. Sim said there would maybe be no need to cottar, though he'd never thought of the thing before, he spent every meck he ever had made on drink and coarse queans, any coarseness at all that didn't trouble his sweirty too much. But now with the grey-eyed quean in his arms he felt as he'd done that time when a loon and he made up his mind he would win the school prize. 'I get a bit place of my own. You'll wait?'

Kate shrugged and said, 'Maybe, you'll have to risk that.' Sim held her and looked at her, suddenly cuddled her, daft and tight till she nearly screamed, just for a minute, and syne finished with that. 'You needn't be feered, I'll wait for my turn. That's just a taste of what I'll yet take. What about a kiss?' And she gave him one, cold, like a peck, but he thought it fine, and lapped it in and put her away, and went swinging away home the Kinraddie road; you could hear him nearly a mile from the bothy, singing as he climbed up the road in the dark.

Well, God! there fair was a change in him then. It was brose and then brose and syne brose to his meat. The other billies in the bothy would laugh, and mock at Sim, and cry, 'What's it all for? But Sim didn't heed, he saved every penny, he worked extra work, and afore two years, what with saving and scraping, he'd enough silver saved for the rent of Haughgreen.

It lies low down by the Segget burn. The clay of the Mearns has thickened down there till in a dry season a man might well think he stood in the yard of a milk-jar potter, the drills just hillocks and slivers of clay. Its rent was low, in spite of its size, the most of the biggings just held together, disheartened-like, as though waiting the time to fall in a rickle on somebody's head. But Sim gave a swagger, 'I'll manage them fine,' the daft-like glaze on his queer green eyes; and was off every night from the Upperhill bothy, not down as afore to Kate Duthie in Segget, but down to Haughgreen with a saw and an axe, pliers and planes, and the Lord knows what. In the last week afore he was due to move in, the Upperhill foreman went down for a look, and he found Haughgreen all shored-up and trig, the house all new-papered, with furniture in it, the stable fit to take horses again, the stalls in the byre set well for nout – he'd worked like a nigger had that sweir brute, Sim.

The foreman said 'twas a miracle, just; he was glad that Sim had wakened at last. Sim gave him a clap that near couped him at that, 'Ay, man, and for why? Because I'll soon have the best quean in the Howe. What think you of that? In my house and my bed!'

That night he tramped to his quean down in Segget, and knocked at the kitchen door of the Manse, and Kate came to it and said, 'Oh, it's you?' And Sim said 'Ay,' with his eyes fit to eat her, 'You mind what I asked you near two years back?'

Kate said, 'What was that?' She thought little of him, and knew nothing of his slaving to save for Haughgreen. But he started to tell her, as he stood in the door, that he was a farmer, with a farm of his own, and ready to take her there when she liked.

She gaped and said, 'Sim, it's not true, is it now?' And he said, 'Ay, it is.' And she fair seemed to thaw, and speired him up hill and down dale all about it, Sim standing and staring at the white of her neck, white, like cream, and he felt like a cat, and licked his lips with a hungry tongue.

Well, she soon said, 'Aye,' she needed no prigging, fore-seeing herself a braw farmer's wife. At the end of the term the two of them married. Sim looked that day as though wedding an angel, not just a quean with a warm, white skin and close grey eyes and a mouth like a mule. Not but that the creature had smiles for the hour, and was awful kind to the ploughmen that čame. She danced with the foreman and said, 'You're a joskin? Maybe my husband will give you a fee?' And the foreman spat, 'Well, would he now, then? But you see I'm particular-like about the mistress.'

She would try to put Sim against him for that, the foreman knew, and keeked over at Sim; and he saw his eyes as they fixed on Kate, hungry and daft, more a glare than a glower. And he suddenly minded Sim back in the bothy, in the days before he had met with this quean, and that speak of his, 'Trauchle the day just to trauchle the morn! But show me a thing that is worth my chave and I'll work you all off the face of the earth!'

Well, he'd gotten the thing, good luck go with him, the foreman thought as he tramped away home, up through the grey of the morning mists, with the bothy lightless and grey in the dawn, leaving Sim with his hard-eyed quean; you hoped he'd not eat her, that's what he'd looked like.

But faith! she survived, fair the kind to do that. Folk gave a bit laugh at the news from Haughgreen, and shook their heads when they heard that Sim, no sooner married, was as sweir as before, taking life cool as ever he had done, in spite of the nagging and prigging of Kate. The ploughing was on; but Sim Wilson's was not, the parks were lucky did they see him by nine, instead of six, when other childes yoked. Even then he'd do little but stand up and gant, or weeber out loud as he sat on a gate.

Now and then a body would cry to him, 'Ay, your ploughing's far back for the season, is't not?' and he'd say, 'Damn the doubt. What o't though it is?' And he'd whistle and stare at the clouds in the Howe, his cat-like eyes a-blink in the sun.

The foreman at last took a taik in about, and Sim was as pleased to see him as though he wasn't new-married, new-buried instead. Kate snapped from the room like an ill-ta'en rat; she didn't like the foreman, he didn't like her. And he thought as he sat and waited his dram it was more than likely that she wore the breeks.

But right soon he was changing his mind about that. As they sat at their dram, him and Sim, she came back. 'It's dark, and it's time you went for the kye.' 'Gang for them yourself,' Sim said, and never turned. 'You enjoy trauchle; well, enjoy some more.'

Kate's face blazed up like a fire with rage, she choked and went out and banged the door. The foreman felt a bit shamed for the quean. Damn't, you could see it wasn't so easy to be married to a sweir, queer brute like Sim; it wouldn't be long that these two together would store the kiln in Haughgreen, you knew.

There were more stammy-gastered than him at the change. For all of a sudden, as the May came in, Sim seemed to wake up and his sweirty went, he was out at all hours at the work of the parks, chaving like daft at his weed-choked drills. The land had lain fallow, he wasn't too late, and afore folk had well gotten over their gape they saw Sim Wilson was having fine crops, manured with the sweat of his own meikle hams. He snored no more in the lithe of a whin and he stopped from ganting by every bit gate.

The reason for that was soon plain to be seen, Kate with a bairn, and the creature soon due. The Upperhill foreman met in with Sim one night as he drove from the mart at Stonehive, and the foreman cried up, 'Ay, man, and how are you?' Sim stopped and cried back, 'Oh, it's you is it, then?

Fine, man, I'm aye fine; I get what I want. Have you heard of the news of what's coming to Haughgreen?'

And he told the foreman of the bairn that was coming, as if half the Howe didn't know about that, his green, glazed eyes all glinting and shining. You'd have though by the way that Sim Wilson spoke 'twas the first bit bairn that had waited for birth in all the windy Howe of the Mearns. He was daft on it, as daft as he had been a wee while before to marry its mother. And the foreman thought, as he wished him luck, there were some that had aye to be looking ahead, and others looked back, and it made little odds, looked you east, looked you west, you'd to work or to die.

Kate had a sore time and let every soul know, but the midwife said that the queer-like thing was the way that that meikle Sim Wilson behaved, not like most of the fathers she ever had known, and she'd known a fell few; they went into three classes – fools, poor fools, and just plain damn fools. Well, the last were mostly the fathers of first-born, they'd wabble at the knees and whiten at the gills and pay no heed to aught but the wife. Sim Wilson was different, with his unco green eyes, 'twas the bairn that took him his first minute in the room. He had it in his arms as ready as you please, and cuddled it, chuckled to it – the great silly sumph – till Kate whined out from the bed where she lay, 'And have you got nothing to say to me now?' And Sim Wilson said, 'Eh? Damn't, Kate, I'd forgotten you!'

An ill-like thing, that, to say to a wife, but that was the way that the brute now behaved; there was nothing he thought on earth worth the price of daddling his bairn up and down in his arms, and swearing she'd winked, and wasn't she a topper? The Upperhill foreman came down for a look, and keeked at the creature, an ordinary bairn, like an ill-boiled swede; but Sim sat and glowered at her, the look in his eyes he'd once turned on Kate ere he'd money to marry. 'Man, but I'll make a braw life for this lass – I'll give her education and make her a lady.'

The foreman said that he thought education was dirt; if ever he had bairns he'd set them to work. Sim laughed in a way that he didn't much like. 'You? Maybe. I was kittled on a different day.'

So the foreman left him, fair angered at that. 'Twas nearly five years ere he saw Sim again, for he moved down the Howe and took a fresh fee, and got married himself, and had bairns of his own. And sometimes he'd mind of that sweir brute, Sim, and the speaks of his in the bothy long syne: 'Well, what's it all for, all your chaving and care?' And when he'd mind that the foreman would laugh, and know that most likely his stomach was wrong.

Though he didn't see Sim he heard now and then of him and his capers down at Haughgreen. Folk told that he'd turned to a slaver, just, he'd fee'd two men and near worked them to death, and himself as well, and long Kate forbye – faith, if she'd thought she did herself well, marrying a farmer and setting up braw, she'd got many a sore heart since her marriage-morn. Sim gave her no help, he wouldn't fee a maid, he was up and out at the blink of dawn, crying his men from their beds to work. He spared neither man nor beast, did Sim; in his four-five years he'd made a fair pile. But he was as ready as ever he had been to blab what he thought, a sneer or a a boast. And he'd tell any soul that would care to listen the why and the wherefore he moiled like a mole. 'It's that lass of mine, Jean – faith, man, she's a topper! I'm to send her to college, away from this soss, and she'll lack for nothing that money can bring.'

And neither she did. It fair was a scandal, folk said, that plain though they ate at Haughgreen the bairn was fed on this dainty and that. Sim had bought the wee wretch the finest of beds, and he'd have her aye dressed like the bairns of gentry. You'd heard afore this of folk daft on a bairn, but he was surely the worst in the Howe. Folk shook their heads, he had better look out, 'twas fell unchancy to show over-plain that you thought over-much of any bit bairn.

And faith! folk weren't far wrong in their speak – the bairn didn't die, she was healthy enough, but just when it came for the time of her schooling, they seemed to wake up to the fact at Haughgreen. She was unco backward and couldn't speak well, and had funny-like ways; she would croon a bit song all the hours of the day, staring up at the hills of the Howe, not caring a fig what she ate or what she wore, only caring to lie in the sun and to sleep.

Sim sent for a specialist out from Dundon and had the bit bairn taken away south, and treated and tested and God knows what. That went on a six months and the cost was a ruin, a time of sore hearts and black looks at Haughgreen. And he well might have spared his time and his silver, she came back just the same – the bairn was a daftie, and the doctors said that so she'd remain, a bairn of three, all the years of her life.

Folk thought it awful, but they gave a bit snicker, 'Ay, what will that fool at the Haugh say now?' Well, he went in a kind of a daze for weeks, but his work didn't slacken as the foreman had thought – when he heard of the thing he had minded long back how Sim had behaved when he married his Kate and found that angel of common enough clay. But slaving was deep in his bones now, and he couldn't well stop though he wished, you supposed. The foreman met him one day at a roup, sneering and boasting as loudly as ever. But there was a look in the queer green eyes as though he were watching for something he'd tint.

He made no mention of the daftie, Jean, that had answered his question, 'What's it all for?' Sun, wind, and the batter of rain in his face – well, he'd settle now as others had done, and take it all for the riddle it was, not a race to be run with a prize at the end.

Then the news got about and you knew in a blink why he'd acted so calm with his firstborn, Jean. His wife had brought another bit bairn in the world, a lassie as well, and fine and strong. And soon's it was born Sim Wilson was crying, 'Is it right in the head, is it right in the head?' The doctor knew neither one way nor the other, but he said, 'Ay, it's fine,' to quieten the fool.

Sim doted on Jess from the day of her birth, promising her all as he'd done with Jean – Jean that now he could hardly bear to look upon, any more than on Kate, his wife, thin and old. She'd fair withered up, had the thin-flanked Kate, except her bit tongue, it could scoriate your skin. But it didn't vex Sim with his daughter Jess, he would stride in the kitchen when he loosened at night, 'Where's ma wee quean?' and Jess would cry 'Here!' Bonny and trig, like a princess dressed, nothing soft about her like that thing in the corner, hunched up and crooning, aye half-way in sleep. She was clever and bright and a favourite at college, Jess, and Sim swore she should háve what she liked, she never need soss with the land and its pleiter, she would marry no joskin, a lady she'd be.

He bled the red clay of Haughgreen near to white, to wring silver from it for Jess and her life, to send her to college and give her brave clothes. Fegs, he was fair a long gait from the days when he'd mock at the land – 'Ay, come and get me – get me if you can – I'm not such a fool!'

The foreman had clean forgot him for years, Sim Wilson the sweir and the fairlies he chased; and when next he did hear he could hardly believe one thing in the tale that came swift up the Howe. That thing was the age of the daughter, Jess. 'Why, the lassie is only a bairn,' he said. But the childe that stopped to pass him the tale said, 'Faith no, man, eighteen if a day. Ay, a real coarse quean, and you cannot but laugh at the nasty whack it is in the mouth for that meikle fool that farms Haughgreen!'

There was nothing unco in the tale when told, the kind of thing had been known to the world since the coming of men – and afore that, no doubt, else all the ill pleiter would have never begun. But for that to happen to the dawtie of Sim! Jess, the student, so haughty and neat, the maid that had led his question so on, up out of the years: 'What's it all for?'

It seems that she carried her shame a long time, and the

creature that found her out was the daftie, Jean. One night when old Sim came home the daftie pointed at her sister, Jess, and giggled and mowed and made slabbering sounds. Sim had paid her no heed a good twenty years, but something in the wrigglings of the creature took him. He cried, 'What's that?' and glowered at his wife, old Kate, with her thinning face and greyed hair.

But Kate knew nothing, like himself she stared at Jess that sat red-faced by the fire. And then while they stared Jess jumped to her feet, weeping, and ran from the room, and they saw – plain enough, the way she was in; they'd been blind.

Old Sim gave a groan as an old horse groans when you drive him his last bit bout up a hill, and stood and stared at the daftie, Jean, that was giggling and fleering there like a bairn, like something tint from his life long syne, in the kitchen quiet as the daylight waned.

FORSAKEN

'Eloi! Eloi! lama sabachthani?'

For a while you could not think at all what strange toun this
was you had come intil, the blash of the lights dazzled your
eyes so long they'd been used to the dark, in your ears were the
shammle and grind and drummle of dreamminded slopes of
earth or of years, your hands moved with a weight as of lead,
draggingly, anciently, so that you glowered down at them in
a kind of grey startlement. And then as you saw the holes where
the nails had been, the dried blood thick on the long brown
palms, and minded back in a flash to that hour, keen and awful,
and the slavering grins on the faces of the Roman soldiers as
they drove the nails into the stinking Yid. That you minded –
but now – now where had you come from that lang hame?

Right above your head some thing towered up with branch-
ing arms in the flow of the lights; and you saw that it was a cross
of stone, overlaid with curlecues, strange, dreich signs, like the
banners of the Roman robbers of men whom you'd preached
against in Zion last night. Some Gentile city they had carried
you to, you supposed, and your lips relaxed to that, thinking of
the Samaritans, of the woman by the well that day whom you'd
blessed – as often you'd blessed, pitifully and angrily, seeing
the filth and the foolishness in folk, but the kindly glimmer of
the spirit as well. Here even in this stour and stench and glare
there would surely be such folk –

It was wee Johnny Tamson saw the Yid first – feuch! there
the nasty creature stood, shoggling backward and forward alow
Mercat Cross, Johnny kenned at once the coarse brute was
drunk same as father was Friday nights when he got his money
from the Broo. So he handed a hack on the shins to Pete Gordon
that was keeking in at a stall near by to see if he could nick a bit

orange. *There's a fortune-teller, let's gang and make faces at him!*

You were standing under the shadow of the Cross and the Friday market was gurling below, but only the two loons had seen you as yet. You saw them come scrambling up the laired steps, one cried *Well, Yid!* and the other had a pluffer in his hand, and he winked and let up with the thing, and ping! on your cheek. But it didn't hurt, though you put up your hand to give it a dight, your hand you hardly felt on your cheek so strange it had grown, your eyen on the loon. Queer that lads had aye been like that, so in Bethlehem long syne you could mind they had been, though you yourself had never been so, staring at books, at the sky, at the wan long trail of some northing star that led the tired herdsmen home. . . .

Johnny Tamson was shoggling backward and forward two steps below where the sheeny stood, he'd fallen to a coarse-like singing now, trying to vex the foreign fortune-teller:

Yiddy-piddy.
He canna keep steady,
He stan's in an auld nichtgoon!

But Pete hadn't used his pluffer again, he felt all watery inside him, like. He cried up *Don't vex the man!* for something hurt when he looked in those eyen, terrible queer eyen, like mother's sometimes, like father's once. . . . *Stop it!* he cried to young Johnny Tamson.

Johnny Tamson pranced down the steps at that and circled round Pete like a fell raised cat. *Who're you telling to stop?* he asked, and Pete felt feared to his shackle-bone, Johnny Tamson was a bigger chap than him. So, because he was awful feared he said *You!* and bashed Johnny Tamson one in the neb, it burst into blood like a cracked ink-bottle and Johnny went stitering back and couped, backerty-gets into the stall they'd been sneaking about five minutes before, waiting a chance to nick an orange. Old Ma Cleghorn turned round at that minute, just as Johnny hit the leg of the stall and down it went with a showd and a bang.

You saw the thing that happened and heard the quarrel of the loons, understood in a flash, had moved down from the steps of the Mercat Cross, but had not moved quick enough, crash went the stall, and there was the boy Pete staring appalled. As you put your hand on his shoulder he gasped, and looked round: *Oh, it's you!* and was suddenly urgent – *Come on!*

The Yid man wouldn't or he couldn't run, but came loping down the Gallowgate fine, Pete breathing and snorting through his nose and looking back at the stouring market din. Syne he looked at the mannie, and stopt, the street dark: *You'll be all right here*, he said to the mannie, *but they'd have blamed you – they aye blame Yids. Well, so long, I'm away home!*

You looked after the loon and stared round you again at the clorted house-walls of the antrin toun. And then because you went all light-headed you leaned up against the wall of the street, your hand at your eyen as the very street skellacht; till someone plucked at your sleeve. . . .

God damn and blast it, just like young Pete, coming belting against you out in the streets as you were tearing home for your tea: *Father, there's a Yid chap up in the close – with a nightgown on, he looks awful queer. – Well, I'm queer myself, I'm away for my tea. – Father, I want you to take him home with us – you're aye taking queer folk home.* . . . So here was Pa, hauled up to speak to the Yid – and a damned queer-looking felly at that, fair starving the creature was by his look.

Ay, then, Comrade!

You saw something in his face you seemed to know from far-off times, in a lowe of sea-water caught by the sun, in a garden at night when the whit owl grew quiet, that awful night in Gethsemane when you couldn't see the way clear at all, when you were only blank, dead afeared. Comrade! You knew him at once, with your hand to your head, to your heart, in greeting.

PETER!

Ay, that's my name. This young nickun here thinks you're no very well. Will you come in by for a dish of tea?

So next you were walking atween the loon and Peter down one dark street and along another and up dark twisting stairs. And at one of those twists the light from the street shone through on the staircase and through on you, and Peter gave a kind of a gasp.

God, man, where was't I kenned you afore?

II

Sick of father and the tosh he piled in the room, books and papers, an undighted hand-press, wasn't room for a quean to do a hand's-turn to get into her outgoing clothes. Mr. Redding had called that evening to Jess: *Miss Gordon, come into the office,* in she'd gone, he was fat, the creash oozed over his collar, and she'd kenned at once when he closed the door the thing he was going to do. And he'd done it, she'd laughed, it hurt, the bloody beast. But she didn't say so, he sweated and loosed her, paiching: *We'll make a night o' it, eh, my Pootsy? I'll pick you up in the car at Mercat Cross.*

Oh, damn! She found herself greeting a bit, not loud, Mother would hear her greeting like a bairn as she minded that. But what else was there for a lassie to do, if she liked bonny things and fine things to eat, and – oh, to be hapt in a fine rug in a car and get a good bed to lie on – even if it was beside that oozing creash in the dark, as it had been afore now. Mind the last time? . . . But she couldn't do anything else, she'd her job to hold on to, a lot of use to find herself sacked, on the Broo, and father with work only now and then and the rest of his time ta'en up with Bolshêviks – he'd be in the jail with it ere all was done, and where would his family be then?

She found the dress and scraped her way intilt, angrily, and heard the whisp-whisp of folk coming in at the kitchen door, wiping their feet on the bass and Mother speaking to them low. She tore the comb through her hair and opened the door and went into the parlour, not heeding them a damn. *Ma –*

You knew that face at once, the long golden throat and the

wide, strange eyen and the looping up of the brightsome hair, your heart was twisted with a sudden memory, remembering her sorrow, her repentance, once, that night when she laved your feet with tears, how she followed through the stour of the suns and days of those moons when you trekked your men to El Kuds, Magdalene, the Magdalene.

She thought, Oh gosh, isn't father just awful? another tink brought into the house, a fright of a fool in an old nightgown. If Mr. Redding saw him I'd never hear the end. . . . And she looked at the Yid with a flyting eye, but feared a bit, something queer about him, as though she'd once seen him, once long back – that was daft, where could she have seen him? *Mother, where's my crocodile shoon?*

Ma was seating the Yid by the fire, poor creature, he'd been out in ill weather enough in that silly sark-like thing that he wore. He looked sore troubled in his mind about something, the Lord kenned what, men were like that, Ma never bothered about their daft minds, and their ploys and palavers and blether of right, wrong and hate and all the rest of the dirt, they were only loons that never grew up and came back still wanting their bruises bandaged. But she thought the Yid was a fine-like stock, for all that, not like some of the creatures – feuch, how they smelt! that Peter would bring from his Bolshevist meetings.

Fegs, lassie, can you no see to the crocodiles yourself – or the alligators either, if it comes to that? Peter was in fair a good humour the night, warming his nieves, steeking and unsteeking them in front of the fire. *Your Ma's to see to the tea for me and this comrade here that young Pete met up by Mercat Cross.*

Jess banged over under the big box bed and found the crocodiles there, oh no, not cleaned, young Pete was a lazy Bulgar, Ma spoiled him, he never did a thing for his meat, there he sat glowering at that Yid, like a gowk, as though the queer creature were some kind of sweetie. . . . Oh Christ, and they've tint the blasted brushes.

She got down on her knees and raxed out the polish, and started to clean, no body speaking, Ma seeing to the smokies above the fire, Pa warming his hands and Pete just staring, the Yid – Jess looked up then and saw him look at her, she stopped and looked back with a glower of her brows and next minute felt suddenly sick and faint. . . . Oh Gosh, that couldn't have happened to her, not *that*, after that night with Redding? She'd go daft, she'd go out and drown herself if there were a kid –

You could see in this room with the wide, strange lum and those folk who only half-minded you suddenly a flash in the Magdalene's eyes. She was minding – minding you and the days when she joined the band, the New Men you led, while you preached again chastity, patience and love. The Magdalene minding, her eyes all alowe, in a minute she'd speak as Peter had spoken –

Peter said *Those smokies have fairly a right fine guff. Up with them, Ma, I've the meeting to gang to. Sit in about, Comrade, and help yourself. Queer I thought I'd once met you afore – Dottlet, folk sometimes get, eh, ay? Do you like two lumps or three in your tea?*

You heard yourself say *None, if you please*, though this was a queer and antrin stuff put into a queer and antrin drink. Yet it warmed you up as you drank it then and ate the smoked fish the woman Martha served, with a still, grave face (you minded her face in other time, before that birling of dust went past).

Pete thought as he ate up his bit of a smoky, *My Yid chap was famisht as Pa would say. Look how he's tearing into the fish. Maybe he'll help me to plane my bookcase after he's finisht.* And he called out loud, they all gave a loup, *Will you help me to plane my bookcase, chap? You were once a joiner and should do it just fine.*

The loon, you saw, knew you – or kenned only that? *How did you ken that I carpentered?*

– *Och, I just kent. Will you help me? Ma, there's Will coming up the stair.*

Jess got to her feet and slipped into the room, and banged the door and stood biting her lips, feared, but not now so feared as she'd been. If that was the thing that had happened

41

to her she kenned a place where they'd see to it. Ugh, it made her shiver, that couldn't be helped, she'd see to the thing in spite of the Yid. . . . Och, she was going clean daft, she supposed, what had the Yid to do with it all? Something queer as he stared at her? If she vexed over every gowk that stared she'd be in a damn fine soss ere long. In a damn fine soss already, oh Gosh! . . .

Will thought as he stepped in and snibbed the door. Hello, another recruit for the Cause. A perfect devil for recruits, old Pa – wish to God he'd get some with some sense and go. And he sighed, fell tired, and nodded to the man that sat in the queer get-up by the table. Looked clean done in, poor devil in that fancy gown of his, some unemployed Lascar up from the Docks trying on the old fortune-telling stunt. . . .

Of him you were hardly sure at all – the thin, cool face and the burning eyes and the body that had a faint twist as it moved. And then you minded – a breathing space, an hour at night on the twilight's edge when the trees stood thin as pencil smoke, wan, against the saffron sky, in a village you rested in as a train went through, gurling camels with loping tails, and a childe bent down from a camel back, in the light, and stared at you with hard, fierce, cool eyes. And they'd told you he was a Sanhedrin man, Saul of Tarsus, a hater and contemner of the New Men you led.

Will, this is a comrade that young Pete found. My son's the secretary of the Communist cell. Would you be one of the Party yourself?

Will thought, Just like Pa, simple as ever. Poor devil of a Yid, of course he'll say *Ay*. . . . But instead the man looked up and stared, and seemed to think, and syne nodded, half doubtful. *All things in common for the glory of God.*

Pa said *Ay, just, that's what I tell Will. But he will not have it you can be religious at all if you're communist, I think that's daft, the two are the same. But he kens his job well enough, I'll say that. Eat up, Comrade, you're taking nothing.*

You thought back on that wild march up on El Kuds and the ancient phrases came soft on your lips as you looked at the bitter, cool face of Saul, and you heard yourself say them aloud in the room. *All things in common in the Kingdom of God, when the hearts of men are changed by light, when sin has ceased to be.*

Will thought, Queer how that delusion still lasts, queer enough in this poor, ragged devil from the Docks. Funny, too, how he said the old, empty words as though they were new and bit and pringled, not the grim, toothless tykes they are. Looked in a funny-like way when he said them, one half-believed one had seen him before. Oh, well, oh hell, couldn't let that pass. Agitprop, even while eating a smoky!

That's been tried and found useless over long, Comrade. Waiting the change of heart, I mean. It's not the heart we want to change, but the system. Skunks with quite normal hearts can work miraculous change for the good of men. People who have themselves changed hearts are generally crucified – like Christ.

– Christ? Who is Christ?

They all glowered at him, Pete fair ashamed, it wasn't fair the poor Yid should be shown up like that. Ma turned to the fire again, Eh me, the Jew felly was unco unlearned, poor brute, with they staring eyen – and whatever had he been doing to those hands of his? Pa reddened and pushed the oat cakes over.

Help yourself, Comrade, you're eating nothing. Never mind about Jesus, he's long been dead.

Jesus? What Jesus was this of theirs, who brought that look of shame to them? Some prophet of antique time, no doubt, this man named as someone you knew had been named. . . . Saul's eyen staring with that question in them – neither the eyen of an enemy nor yet of a frere.

Who was Jesus?

Ma thought, Well, well, and now they'll be at it. Will'll never get his smoky down at all with all this blether he's having on hand telling the poor Jew man about Jesus – Eh me, and the way he speaks, too, right bonny, though no very decent my mother'd have thought. But that was long syne, afore you met in with Peter Gordon and his queer-like notions –

scandalized mother off the earth, near, they had! . . . *Will, would you have another smoky?*

– No, Ma, thank you kindly. . . . So that was the way of it, you see, this Prophet childe started with the notion that men's hearts would first need changing, to make them love one another, care for the State – he called it the Kingdom of God in his lingo. And what happened was that he himself was crucified after leading an army against Jerusalem; syne, hardly was he dead than his followers started making a god of him, quite the old kind of God, started toning down all he'd taught to make it fit in with the structure of the Roman state. They became priests and princes in the service of the temples dedicated to the dead Jesus, whom they'd made a God. . . . And, mind you, that change of heart must have happened often enough to folk when they heard of the sayings of this Jesus. Thousands and thousands changed – but there was no cohesion – no holding together, they put off the Kingdom of God till Eternity: and were tortured and murdered in Jesus' name.

You stared in the bright sharp eyes of Saul and saw now that he had no knowledge of you. Jesus? – many years ago, he had said. . . . And after that last black night, that hour when you cried to God forsaking you, mad darkness had descended again on the earth, on the faces and souls of Magdalene and Martha, Peter and Saul – Peter there with the old, kind smile on his face, his mind far lost in dreams. And those banners you had led up the passes against El Kuds were put away for the flaunting flag of a God – a God worshipped afar in the strange touns.

Ma cried, *Eh, mighty, the poor child's no well. Lean back a minute; Pete, open that window; Fegs you fair gave me a turn, man!*

III

Jess Gordon came out from the room all dressed, with her crocodiles on, as they tended the Yid. He opened his eyen as she stepped in the room, Gosh, what need had he to look at her like that, as though he both *kenned* and nearly grat? Well, she didn't care, not a damn, she was going out with Redding,

44

she would tell them all that, that greasy Lascar into the bargain. *What's wrong with him, Ma?*

And now you saw she was not the Magdalene – or the Magdalene after two thousand years with the steel of a Roman sword in her heart, sharper, clearer, colder than of yore, not to be moved by glance or touch or the aura of God that you carried from those Bethlehem days as a loon. This was Magdalene from the thousands of years that drummlet and rumblet into the night since the pain tore deep in your wounded feet. . . .

Ma said, *The childe was feeling the heat, just don't vex him and don't stare at him like that, as though he had done you some ill or other. And where are you off to with your crocodiles on?*

– *To meet a chap if you want to know.* Jess dragged her eyen from those staring eyen. (Damn him, he could stare.) *Ta-ta, folk.*

Ta, ta, they called. She turned at the door. *And ta-ta, YOU.* Her look was a knife.

Pa louped up as she banged the door. *What's ta'en the ill-getted bitch the night? Glowering that way at the Comrade here? . . . Eh, what did you say?*

You had said only *Peter!* and at that he had turned, for a moment you saw loup into his eyen that love and amazement that had once been his, love and amazement for the leader, not the creed, it died away as he sat down again. And even he you saw now was not the Peter of that other time, weak and leal and kind he had been, but more of the kindness now, little of the love, forsaken of the trust and uttermost belief. No thing in him now you could ever touch except with a cry of despair.

Ma said, *There was nothing to fuss about. Finish your tea, you've your meeting, Pa. Pete, it's time you were off to your bed. Say ta-ta now to the gentlemen.*

– *Och, isn't there no time for my bookcase, Ma? All right, all right, ta-ta, chap.*

The mannie looked and said *Ta-ta.* And again something

came twisting in young Pete's wame. He looked back, white-faced, from the bedroom door. *Ta-ta. I – liked you awful, you ken.*

– *Hear that?* said Pa. *He's fair ta'en to you, Comrade. Well, I'll need t'away to the meeting, I doubt. You'll be down there, Will?*

– *Ay will I, worse luck. Is the comrade coming?*

You looked from the face of one to the other, the faces of Martha and Saul and Peter, and you saw, no mist now happing your eyen (that mist from past times), they'd no kinship with you. Saul with the bitter face and creed, a leader once for that army you led up the heights to El Kuds, never for that love you had led it with. Looking into his heart with that ancient power you saw the white, stainless soul that was there, but love had gone from it, faith and trust, hope even, only resolve remained. Nothing there but resolve, nothing else that survived the awful torment your name had become. . . . And you saw in the face of Martha even something that was newer or older than you – a cold and a strange and a terrible thing, a mother of men with the eyen of men, facing fear and pain without hope as did Saul, wary and cool, un-bannered, unafraid. . . . You shook your head:

No. I maun gang to my hame.

They could never make up their minds what he said next, that minute when he covered his face with his hands, afore he went out of the house and their lives. Pa said it was something about some Eliot, Will said the poor Lascar devil had mumbled something or other about the Sabbath.

CLAY

The Galts were so thick on the land around Segget folk said
if you went for a walk at night and you trod on something
and it gave a squiggle, it was ten to one you would find it a
Galt. And if you were a newcomer up in the Howe and you
stopped a man and asked him the way, the chances were he'd
be one of the brood. Like as not, before he had finished with
you, he'd have sold you a horse or else stolen your watch,
found out everything that you ever had done, recognised
your mother and had doubts of your father. Syne off home
he'd go and spread the news round, from Galt of Catcraig
that lay high in the hills to Galt of Drumbogs that lay low
by Mondynes, all your doings were known and what you had
said, what you wore next your skin what you had to your
breakfast, what you whispered to your wife in the dead of
the night. And the Galts would snigger *Ay, gentry, no doubt,*
and spit in the vulgar way that they had: the average Galt
knew less of politeness than a broody hen knows of Bible
exegesis.

They farmed here and they farmed there, brothers and
cousins and half-brothers and uncles, your head would reel
as you tried to make out if Sarah were daughter to Ake of
Catcraig or only a relation through marrying a nephew of
Sim of High Rigs that was cousin to Will. But the Galts knew
all their relationships fine, more especially if anything had
gone a bit wrong, they'd tell you how twenty-five years or
so back, when the daughter of Redleaf had married her
cousin, old Alec that now was the farmer of Kirn, the first
bit bairn that came of that marriage – ay, faith, that bairn
had come unco soon! And they'd lick at their chops as they
minded of that and sneer at each other and fair have a time.

47

But if you were strange and would chance to agree, they'd close up quick, with a look on their faces as much as to say *And who are you would say ill of the Galts?*

They made silver like dirt wherever they sat, there was hardly a toun that they sat in for long. So soon's they moved in to some fresh bit farm they'd rive up the earth, manure it with fish, work the land to death in the space of their lease, syne flit to the other side of the Howe, with the land left dry as a rat-sucked swede. And often enough, as he neared his lease-end, a Galt would break and be rouped from his place, he'd say that farming was just infernal, and his wife would weep as she watched her bit things sold here and there to cover their debts. And if you didn't know much of the Galts you would be right sorry and would bid fell high. Syne you'd hear in less than a six months' time that the childe that went broke had bought a new farm and had stocked it up to the hilt with the silver he'd laid cannily by before he went broke.

Well, the best of the bunch was Rob Galt of Drumbogs, lightsome and hearty, not mean like the rest, he'd worked for nearly a twenty-five years as his father's foreman up at Drumbogs. Old Galt, the father, seemed nearly immortal, the older he grew the coarser he was, Rob stuck the brute as a good son should, though aye he had wanted land of his own. When they fell out at last Rob Galt gave a laugh, *You can keep Drumbogs and all things that are on it, I'll soon get a place of my own, old man.* His father sneered *You?* and Rob Galt said *Ay, a place of my own and parks that are MINE.*

He was lanky and long like all of the Galts, his mouser twisted up at the ends, with a chinny Galt face and a long, thin nose, and eyes pale-blue in a red-weathered face, a fine, frank childe that was kindness itself, though his notion of taking a rest from the plough was to loosen his horses and start in to harrow. He didn't look long for a toun of his own, Pittaulds by Segget he leased in a wink, it stood high up on the edge of the Mounth, you could see the clutter of Segget below, wet, with the glint of its roofs at dawn. The rent was low, for the land was coarse, red clay that sucked with a hungry mouth at your feet as you passed through the evening fields.

Well, he moved to Pittaulds in the autumn term, folk watched his flitting come down by Mondynes, and turn at the corner and trudge up the brae to the big house poised on the edge of the hill. He brought his wife, she was long as himself, with a dark-like face, quiet, as though gentry – faith, that was funny, a Galt wedded decent! But he fair was fond of the creature, folk said, queer in a man with a wife that had managed to bring but one bairn into the world. That bairn was now near a twelve years old, dark, like her mother, solemn and slim, Rob spoiled them both, the wife and the quean, you'd have thought them sugar he was feared would melt.

But they'd hardly sat down a week in Pittaulds when Rachel that would trot at the rear of Rob, like a collie dog, saw a queer-like change. Now and then her father would give her a pat, and she'd think that he was to play as of old. But instead he would cry *Losh, run to the house, and see if your mother will let you come out, we've two loads of turnips to pull afore dinner.* Rachel, the quean, would chirp out *Ay, father,* and go blithe to the shed for her tailer and his, and out they would wade through the cling of the clay and pull side by side down the long, swede rows, the rain in a drifting seep from the hills, below them the Howe in its garment of mist. And the little, dark quean would work by his side, say never a word though she fair was soaked; and at last go home; and her mother would stare, whatever in the world had happened to Rob? She would ask him that as he came into dinner – *the quean'll fair have her death of cold.* He would blink with his pale-blue eyes, impatient, *Hoots, lassie, she'll take no harm from the rain. And we fair must clear the swedes from the land, I'm a good three weeks behind with the work.*

The best of the Galts? Then God keep off the rest! For, as that year wore on to its winter, while he'd rise at five, as most other folk did, he wouldn't be into his bed till near morning, it was chave, chave, chave till at last you would think he'd turn himself into an earthworm, near. In the blink of the light from the lanterns of dawn he would snap short-tempered at his dark-faced wife, she would stare and wonder and give a bit laugh, and eat up his porridge as though he was feared he would lose his appetite halfway through, and muck out the byre and the stable as fast as though he were paid for the job by the hour, with a scowl of ill-nature behind his long nose. And then, while the dark still lay on the land, and through the low mist that slept on the fields, not a bird was cheeping and not a thing showing but the waving lanterns in the Segget wynds, he'd harness his horses and lead out the first, its hooves striking fire from the stones of the close, and cry to the second, and it would come after, and the two of them drink at the trough while Rob would button up his collar against the sharp drive of the frozen dew as the north wind woke. Then he'd jump on the back of the meikle roan, Jim, and go swaying and jangling down by the hedge, in the dark, the world on the morning's edge, wet, the smell of the parks in his face, the squelch of the horses soft in the clay.

Syne, as the light came grey in a tide, wan and slow, from the Bervie Braes, and a hare would scuttle away through the grass, and the peesies waken and cry and wheep, Rob Galt would jump from the back of Jim, and back the pair up against the plough, and unloose the chains from the horses' britchens and hook them up to the swiveltrees. Then he'd spit on his hands and cry *Wissh, Jim!* no longer ill-natured, but high-out and pleased, and swink the plough into the red, soaked land; and the horses would strain and snort and move canny, and the clay wheel back in the coulter's trace, Rob swaying slow in the rear of the plough, one foot in the drill and one on the rig. The bothy billies on Arbuthnott's bents, riding their pairs to start on some park, would cry one to the other, *Ay, Rob's on the go*, seeing him then as the light grew strong, wheeling, him and his horses and plough, a ranging of dots on the park that sloped by its long clay rigs to the edge of the moor.

By eight, as Rachel set out for school, a slim, dark thing with her well-tacked boots, she would hear the whistle of her father, Rob, deep, a wheeber, up on the hill; and she'd see him come swinging to the end of a rig, and mind how he once would stop and would joke, and tease her for lads that she had at the school. And she'd cry *Hello, father!* but Rob would say nothing till he'd drawn his horse out and looked back at the rig, and given his mouser a twist and a wipe. Syne he'd peek at his daughter as though he'd new woke, *Ay, then, so you're off,* and cry *Wissh!* to his horses and turn them about, and set to again, while Rachel went on, quiet, with the wonder clouding her face that had altered so since she came to Pittaulds.

He'd the place all ploughed ere December was out, folk said that he'd follow the usual Galt course, he'd showed up mean as the rest of them did, he'd be off to the marts and a dealing in horses, or a buying of this or a stealing of that, if there were silver in the selling of frogs the Galts would puddock-hunt in their parks. But instead he began on the daftest-like ploy, between the hill of Pittaulds and the house a stretch of the moor thrust in a thin tongue, three or four acre, deep-pitted with holes and as rank with whins as a haddock with scales, not a tenant yet who had farmed Pittaulds but had had the sense to leave it a-be. But Rob Galt set in to break up the land, he said it fair cried to have a man at it, he carted great stones to fill up the holes, and would lever out the roots when he could with a pick, when he couldn't he'd bring out his horses and yoke them, and tear them out from the ground that way. Working that Spring to break in the moor, by April's end he was all behind, folk took a laugh, it served the fool fine.

Once in a blue moon or so he'd come round, he fair was a deave as he sat by your fire, he and your man would start in on the crops, and the lie of the land, and how you should drain it, the best kind of turnips to plant in the clay, the manure that would bring the best yield a dry year. Your man would be keen enough on all that, but not like Rob Galt, he would kittle up daft, and start in to tell you tales of the land that were just plain stite, of this park and that as though they were women you'd to prig and to pat afore they'd come on. And your man would go ganting wide as a gate, and the clock would be hirpling the hours on to morn, and still Rob Galt would sit there and habber, *Man, she's fairly a bitch, is that park, sly and sleeked, you can feel it as soon as you start in on her, she'll take corn with the meikle husk, not with the little. But I'll kittle her up with some phosphate, I think.* Your man would say *Ay, well, well, is that so? What do you think of this business of Tariffs?* and Rob would say *Well, man, I just couldn't say. What worries me's that park where I've put in the tares. It's fair on the sulk about something or other.*

And what could you think of a fool like that? Though he'd fallen behind with his chave on the moor, he soon made it up with his working at night, he fair had a fine bit crop the next year, the wife and the quean both out at the cutting, binding and stooking as he reapered the fields. Rachel had shot up all of a sudden, you looked at her in a kind of surprise as you saw the creature go by to the school. It was said that she fair was a scholar, the quean – no better than your own bit Johnnie, you knew, the teachers were coarse to your Johnnie, the tinks. Well, Rachel brought home to Pittaulds some news the night that Rob came back from the mart, he'd sold his corn at a fair bit price. For once he had finished pleitering outside, he sat in the kitchen, his feet to the fire, puffing at his pipe, his eye on the window, watching the ley rise up outside and peer in the house as though looking for him. It was Rachel thought that, as she sat at her supper, dark, quiet, a bit queer, over thin to be bonny, you like a lass with a good bit of beef. Well, she finished her meat and syne started to tell the message the Dominie had sent her home with; and maybe if she was sent to the college she'd win a bursary or something to help.

Her mother said *Well, Rob, what say you to that?* and Rob

asked *What?* and they told him again, and Rob skeughed his face round, *What, money for school? And where do you think that I'll manage to get that?*

Mrs Galt said *Out of the corn you've just sold,* and Rob gave a laugh as though speaking to a daftie – *I've my seed to get, and my drains to dig, and what about the ley for the next year's corn? Damn't, it's just crying aloud for manure, it'll hardly leave me a penny-piece over.*

Rachel sat still and looked out at the ley, sitting so, still, with her face in the dark. Then they heard her sniff and Rob swung round, fair astonished-like at the sound she made. *What ails you?* he asked, and her mother said *Ails her? You would greet yourself if you saw your life ruined.* Rob got to his feet and gave Rachel a pat. *Well, well, I'm right sorry that your taking't like that. But losh, it's a small bit thing to greet over. Come out and we'll go for a walk round the parks.*

So Rachel went with him, half-hoping he thought to change his mind on this business of college. But all that he did on the walk was to stand now and then and stare at the flow of the stubble, or laugh queer-like as they came to a patch where the grass was bare and the crop had failed. *Ay, see that, Rachel, the wretch wouldn't take. She'll want a deep drill, this park, the next season.* And he bent down and picked up a handful of earth, and trickled the stuff through his fingers, slow, then dusted it back on the park, not the path, careful, as though it were gold-dust, not dirt. So they came at last to the moor he had broken, he smoked his pipe and he stood and looked at it, *Ay, quean, I've got you in fettle at last.* He was speaking to the park, not his daughter, but Rachel hated Pittaulds from that moment, she thought, quiet, watching her father and thinking how much he'd changed since he first set foot on its clay.

He worked from dawn until dark, and still later, he hove great harvests out of the land, he was mean as dirt with the silver he made; but in five years' time of his farming there he'd but hardly a penny he could call his own. Every meck that he got from the crops of one year seemed to cry to go back to the crops of the next. The coarse bit moor that lay north of the biggings he coddled as though 'twas his own blood and bone, he fed it manure and cross-ploughed twice-thrice, and would harrow it, tend it, and roll the damn thing till the Segget joke seemed more than a joke, that he'd take it to bed with him if he could. For all that his wife saw of him in hers he might well have done that, Mrs Galt, that was tall and dark and so quiet, came to look at him queer as he came in by, you could hardly believe it still was the Rob that once wouldn't blush to call you his jewel, that had many a time said all he wanted on earth was a wife like he had and land of his own. But that was before he had gotten the land.

One night she said as they sat at their meat *Rob, I've still that queer pain in my breast. I've had it for long and I doubt that it's worse. We'll need to send for the doctor, I think.* Rob said *Eh?* and gleyed at her dull, *Well, well, that's fine, I'll need to be stepping, I must put in a two-three hours the night on the weeds that are coming so thick in the swedes, it's fair pestered with the dirt, that poor bit of a park.* Mrs Galt said *Rob, will you leave your parks, just for a minute, and consider me? I'm ill and I want a doctor at last.*

Late the next afternoon he set off for Stonehive, and the light came low and the hours went by, Mrs Galt saw nothing of her man or the doctor, and near went daft with the worry and pain. But at last as it grew fell black on the fields she heard the step of Rob on the close, and she ran out and cried *What's kept you so long?* and he said *What's that? Why, what but my work?* He'd come back and he'd seen his swedes waiting the hoe, so he'd got off his bike and held into the hoeing, what sense would there have been in wasting his time going up to the house to tell the news that the doctor wouldn't be till the morn?

Well, the doctor came in his long brown car, he cried to Rob as he hoed the swedes, *I'll need you up at the house with me.* And Rob cried *Why? I've no time to waste.* But he got at last into the doctor's car, and drove to the house, and waited impatient; and the doctor came ben, and was stroking his

54

lips; and he said *Well, Galt, I'm feared I've bad news. Your wife has a cancer in the breast, I think.*

She'd to take to her bed and was there a good month while Rob Galt worked the Pittaulds on his own. Syne she wrote a letter to her daughter Rachel that was fee'd in Segget, and Rachel came home. And she said, quiet, *Mother, has he never looked near you? I'll get the police on the beast for this,* she meant her own father that was out with the hay, through the window she could see him scything a bout, hear the skirl of the stone as he'd whet the wet blade, the sun a still lowe on the drowsing Howe, the dying woman in the littered bed, But Mrs Galt whispered. *He just doesn't think, it's not that he's cruel, he's just mad on Pittaulds.*

But Rachel was nearly a woman by then, dark, quiet, with a temper that all the lads knew, and she hardly waited for her father to come home to tell him how much he might well be ashamed, he had nearly killed her mother with neglect, was he just a beast and with no heart at all? But Rob hardly looked at the quean in his hurry, *Hoots, lassie, your stomach's gone sour with the heat. Could I leave my parks to get covered with weeds?* And he gave her a pat, as to quieten a bairn, and ate up his dinner, all in a fash to be coling the hay. Rachel cried *Aren't you going to look in on mother?* and he said *Oh, ay,* and went ben in a hurry, *Well, lass, you'll be pleased that the hay's done fine. – Damn't there's a cloud coming up from the sea!* And the next that they saw he was out of the house, staring at the cloud as at Judgment Day.

Mrs Galt was dead ere September's end, on the day of the funeral as folk came up they met Rob Galt in his old cord breeks, with a hoe in his hand, and he said he'd been out loosening up the potato drills a wee bit. He changed to his black and he helped with his brothers to carry the coffin out to the hearse. There were three bit carriages, he got in the first, and the horses went jangling slow to the road. The folk in the carriage kept solemn and long-faced, they thought Rob the same because of his wife. But he suddenly woke, *Damn't man, but I've got it! It's LIME that I should have given the yavil. It's been greeting for the stuff, that park on the brae.*

Rachel took on the housekeeping job at Pittaulds, quiet, dark as her mother, aye reading in books, she would stand of a winter night and listen to the suck and slob of the rain on the clay, and hated the sound as she tried to hate Rob. And sometimes he'd say as they sat at their meat *What's wrong with you, lass, that you're glowering like that?* and the quean would look down, and remember her mother, while Rob rose cheery and went to his work.

And yet, as she told to one of the lads that came cycling up from Segget to see her, she just couldn't hate him, hard though she tried. There was something in him that tugged at herself, daft-like, a feeling with him that the fields mattered and mattered, nothing else at all. And the lad said *What, not even me, Rachel?* and she laughed and gave him that which he sought, but half-absent like, she thought little of lads.

Well, that winter Rob Galt made up his mind that he'd break in another bit stretch of the moor, beyond the bit he already had broke, there the land rose steep in a birn of wee braes, folk told him he fair would be daft to break that. It was land had lain wild and unfed since the Flood. Rob Galt said *Maybe, but they're queer-like, those braes, as though some childe had once shored them tight up.* And he set to the trauchle as he'd done before, he'd come sweating in like a bull at night, and Rachel would ask him *Why don't you rest?* and he'd stare at her dumbfoundered a moment, *What, rest, and me with my new bit park? What would I do but get on with my work?*

And then, as the next day wore to its close, she heard him crying her name outbye, and went through the close, and he waved from the moor. So she closed the door and went up by the track through the schlorich of the wet November moor, a windy day on the winter's edge, the hills a-cower from the bite of the wind, the whins in that wind had a moan as they moved, not a day for a dog to be out, you would say. But she found her father near tirred to the skin, he'd been heaving a great root up from its hold, *Come in by and look on this fairely, lass, I knew that some childe had once farmed up here.*

And Rachel looked at the hole in the clay, and the chamber behind it, dim in the light, where there gleamed a rickle of stone-grey sticks, the bones of a man of antique time. Amid the bones was a litter of flints and a crumbling stick in the shape of a heuch.

She knew it as an eirde of olden time, an earth-house built by the early folk, Rob nodded, *Ay, he was more than that. Look at that heuch, it once scythed Pittaulds. Losh, lass I'd have liked to have kenned that childe, what a crack together we'd have had on the crops!*

Well, that night Rob started to splutter and hoast, next morning was over stiff to move, fair clean amazed at his own condition. Rachel got a neighbour to go for the doctor, Rob had taken a cold while he stood and looked at the hole and the bones in the old-time grave. There was nothing in that and it fair was a shock when folk heard the news in a two-three days Rob Galt was dead of the cold he had took. He'd worked all his go in the ground, nought left to fight the black hoast that took hold of his lungs.

He'd said hardly a word, once whispered *The Ley,* the last hour as he lay and looked out at that park, red-white, with a tremor of its earthen face as the evening glow came over the Howe. Then he said to Rachel *You'll take on the land, you and some childe, I've a notion for that?* But she couldn't lie even to please him just then, she'd no fancy for either the land or a lad, she shook her head and Rob's gley grew dim.

When the doctor came in he found Rob dead, with his face to the wall and the blinds down-drawn. He asked the quean if she'd stay there alone, all the night with her father's corpse? She nodded, *Oh, yes,* and watched him go, standing at the door as he drove off to Segget. Then she turned her about and went up through the parks, quiet, in the wet, quiet gloaming's coming, up through the hill to the old earth-house.

There the wind came sudden in a gust in her hair as she looked at the place and the way she had come, and thought of the things the minister would say when she told him she planned her father be buried up here by the bones of the man of old time. And she shivered sudden as she looked round about, at the bare clay slopes that slept in the dusk, the whistle of the whins seemed to rise in a voice, the parks below to whisper and listen as the wind came up them out of the east.

All life – just clay that awoke and strove to return again to its mother's breast. And she thought of the men who had made these rigs, and the windy days of their toil and years, the daftness of toil that had been Rob Galt's, that had been that of many men long on the land, though seldom seen now, was it good, was it bad? What power had that been that woke once on this brae and was gone at last from the parks of Pittaulds?

For she knew in that moment that no other would come to tend the ill rigs in the north wind's blow. This was finished and ended, a thing put by, and the whins and the broom creep down once again, and only the peesies wheep and be still when she'd gone to the life that was hers, that was different, and the earth turn sleeping, unquieted no longer, her hungry bairns in her hungry breast, where sleep and death and the earth were one.

ESSAYS

THE ANTIQUE SCENE

The history of Scotland may be divided into the three phases of Colonization, Civilization, and Barbarization. That the last word is a synonym for Anglicization is no adverse reflection upon the quality of the great English culture. Again and again, in the play of the historic forces, a great civilization imposed on an alien and lesser has compassed that alien's downfall.

Few things cry so urgently for rewriting as does Scots history, in few aspects of her bastardized culture has Scotland been so ill-served as by her historians. The chatter and gossip of half the salons and drawing-rooms of European intellectualism hang over the antique Scottish scene like a malarial fog through which peer the fictitious faces of heroic Highlanders, hardy Norsemen, lovely Stewart queens, and dashing Jacobite rebels. Those stage-ghosts shamble amid the dimness, and mope and mow in their ancient parts with an idiotic vacuity but a maddening persistence. Modern research along orthodox lines balks from the players, or re-names them shyly and retires into footnotes on Kaltwasser.

Yet behind those grimaces of the romanticized or alien imagination a real people once lived and had its being, and hoped and feared and hated, and was greatly uplifted, and loved its children, and knew agony of the patriotic spirit, and was mean and bestial, and generous, and sardonically merciful. Behind the posturings of those poltergeists are the lives of millions of the lowly who wiped the sweats of toil from browned faces and smelt the pour of waters by the Mull of Kintyre and the winds of autumn in the Grampian haughs and the sour, sweet odours of the upland tarns; who tramped in their varying costumes and speeches to the colour and play of the old guild-towns; who made great poetry and sang it; who begat their kind in shame or delight in the begetting; who were much as you or I, human animals bedevilled or uplifted by the play of the forces of civilization in that remote corner of the Western world which we call Scotland.

All human civilizations originated in Ancient Egypt. Through the accident of time and chance and the cultivation of wild barley in the Valley of the Nile, there arose in a single spot on the earth's surface the urge in men to upbuild for their economic salvation the great fabric of civilization. Before the planning of that architecture enslaved the minds of men, man was a free and happy and undiseased animal wandering the world in the Golden Age of the poets (and reality) from the Shetlands to Tierra del Fuego. And from that central focal point in Ancient Egypt the first civilizers spread abroad the globe the beliefs and practices, the diggings and plantings and indignations and shadowy revilements of the Archaic Civilization.

They reached Scotland in some age that we do not know, coming to the Islands of Mist in search of copper and gold and pearls, Givers of Life in the fantastic theology that followed the practice of agriculture. They found the Scots lowlands and highlands waving green into morning and night tremendous forests where the red deer bellowed, where the great bear, perhaps, had still his tracks and his caverns, where wolves howled the hills in great scattering packs, where, in that forested land, a danker climate than to-day prevailed. And amid those forests and mountain slopes lived the Golden Age hunters – men perhaps mainly of Maglemosian stock, dark and sinewy and agile, intermixed long ages before with other racial stocks, the stock of Cro-Magnard and Magdalenian who had followed the ice-caps north when the reindeer vanished from the French valleys. They were men naked, cultureless, without religion or social organization, shy hunters, courageous, happy, kindly, who stared at the advent of the first great boats that brought the miners and explorers of the Archaic Civilization from Crete or Southern Spain. They flocked down to stare at the new-comers, to offer tentative gifts of food and the like; and to set on their necks the yoke under which all mankind has since passed.

For the Archaic Civilization rooted in Scotland. Agriculture was learned from the Ancient Mariners and with it the host of rites deemed necessary to propitiate the gods of the earth and the sky. Village communities came into being, the first peasants with the first overlords, those priestly overlords who built the rings of the Devil Stones on the high places from Lewis to Aberdeenshire. And the ages came and passed and the agricultural belts grew and spread, and the smoke of sacrifice rose from a thousand altars through the length and breadth of the land at the times of seedtime and harvest, feast and supplication. They buried their dead in modifications of the Egyptian fashion, in Egyptian graves. There came to them, in the slow ebb of the centuries, a driftage of other cultural elements from that ferment of civilization in the basin of the Mediterranean. They learned their own skill with stick and stone, presently with copper, and at last with bronze. But, until the coming of the makers of bronze that Archaic civilization in Scotland, as elsewhere, was one singularly peaceful and undisturbed. Organized warfare had yet to dawn on the Western World.

How it dawned is too lengthy a tale to tell here in any detail: how bands of forest-dwellers in the Central European areas, uncivilized, living on the verge of the great settlements of the Archaic communities and absorbing little but the worst of their practices, fell on those communities and murdered them was the first great tragedy of pre-Christian Europe. The ancient matriarchies of the Seine were wiped from existence and in their place, (and presently across the Channel) came swarming the daggerarmed hosts of a primitive who, never civilized, had become a savage. This was the Kelt.

We see his advent in the fragments of sword and buckler that lie ticketed in our museums; but all the tale of that rape of a civilization by the savage, far greater and infinitely more tragic than the rape of the Roman Empire by the Goth, is little more than a faint moan and murmur in the immense cañons of near-history. In Scotland, no doubt, he played his characteristic part, the Kelt, coming armed on a peaceful population, slaying and robbing and finally enslaving, establishing himself as king and overlord, routing the ancient sun-priests from the holy places and establishing his own devil-haunted, uneasy myths and gods through the efforts of the younger sons. From Berwick to Cape Wrath the scene for two hundred years must have been a weary repetition, year upon year, of invasion and murder, inversion and triumph. When Pytheas sailed the Scottish coasts it is likely that the Kelt had triumphed almost everywhere. By the time the Romans came raiding across the English Neck Scotland was a land of great barbaric Kelt tribes, armed and armoured, with a degenerate, bastardized culture and some skill in war and weapon-making. It was as capable of producing a ferocious soldiery and a great military leader like Calgacus as it was incapable of a single motif in art or song to influence the New Civilization of the European World.

Yet of that culture of those Picts or Painted Men, those Caledonians whom the Romans encountered and fought and marvelled upon, it is doubtful if a single element of any value had been contributed by the Kelt. It is doubtful if the Kelts ever contributed a single item to the national cultures of the countries miscalled Keltic. It is doubtful for the best of reasons : there is no proof that the Kelts, invading Britain, came in any great numbers. They were a conquering military caste, not a people in migration : they imposed their language and their social organization upon the basic Maglemosian-Mediterranean stock ; they survived into remoter times, the times of Calgacus, the times of Kenneth MacAlpin, as nobles, an aristocracy on horseback. They survive to the present day as a thin strand in the Scottish population : half Scotland's landed gentry is by descent Normanized Kelt. But the Kelts are a strain quite alien to the indubitable and original Scot. They were, and remain, one of the greatest curses of the Scottish scene, quick, avaricious, unintelligent, quarrelsome, cultureless, and uncivilizable. It is one of the strangest jests of history that they should have given their name to so much that is fine and noble, the singing of poets and the fighting of great fights, in which their own actual part has been that of gaping, unintelligent audition or mere carrionbird raiding.

The first serious modification of the basic Pictish stock did not occur until towards the end of the sixth Christian century, when the Northumbrian Angles flowed upwards, kingdom-building, as far as the shores of the Firth of Forth. They were a people and nation in transit; they exterminated or reduced to villeinage the Kelt-led Picts of those lands: they succeeded in doing those things not because they were braver or more generous or God-inspired than the Pictish tribes, but because of the fact that they were backed by the Saxon military organization, their weapons were better, and apparently they fronted a congeries of warring tribes inanely led in the usual Keltic fashion – tribes which had interwarred and raided and murdered and grown their crops and drunk their ale unstirred by alien adventures since the passing of the Romans. The Angle pressed north, something new to the scene, bringing his own distinctive culture and language, his own gods and heroes and hero-myths. About the same time a tribe of Kelt-led Irish Mediterraneans crossed in some numbers into Argyllshire and allied themselves with, or subdued the ancient inhabitants. From that alliance or conquest arose the kingdom of Dalriada – the Kingdom of the Scots. Yet this Irish invasion had no such profound effect on the national culture as the coming of the Angles in the South: the Irish Scots were of much the same speech and origin as the Argyllshire natives among whom they settled.

With the coming of the Angles, indeed, the period of Colonization comes to a close. It is amusing to note how modern research disposes of the ancient fallacies which saw Scotland overrun by wave after wave of conquering, colonizing peoples. Scotland was colonized only twice – once fairly completely, once partially, the first time when the Maglemosian hunters drifted north, in hunting, happy-go-lucky migration; the second time, when the Angles lumbered up into Lothian. The Kelt, the Scot, the Norseman, the Norman were no more than small bands of raiders and robbers. The peasant at his im- memorial toil would lift his eyes to see a new master installed at the broch, at the keep, at, later, the castle: and would shrug the matter aside as one of indifference, turning, with the rain in his face, to the essentials of existence, his fields, cattle, his woman in the dark little eirde, earth-house.

The three hundred years after that almost simultaneous descent of Scot and Angle on different sectors of the Scottish scene is a tangle of clumsy names and loutish wars. Kings bickered and bred and murdered and intrigued, armies marched and counter-marched and perpetrated heroisms now dust and nonsense, atrocities the dried blood of which are now not even dust. Christianity came in a number of guises, the Irish heresy a chill blink of light in its coming. It did little or nothing to alter the temper of the times, it was largely a matter of politics and placeseeking, Columba and John Knox apart there is no ecclesiastic in Scots history who does not but show up in the light of impartial research as either a posturing ape, rump-scratching in search of soft living, or as a moronic dullard, hag-ridden by the grisly transplanted fears of the Levant. The peasant merely exchanged the bass chanting of the Druid in the pre-Druid circles for the whining hymnings of priests in wood-built churches; and turned to his land again.

But presently, coastwise, north, west, and east, a new danger was dragging him in reluctant levies from his ancient pursuits. This was the coming of the Norsemen.

If the Kelts were the first great curse of Scotland, the Norse were assuredly the second. Both have gathered to themselves in the eyes of later times qualities and achievements to which the originals possessed no fragment of a claim. The dreamy, poetic, God-moved Kelt we have seen as a mere Chicagoan gangster, murderous, avaricious, culturally sterile, a typical aristocrat, typically base. The hardy, heroic Norseman uncovers into even sorrier reality. He was a farmer or fisherman, raiding in order to supplement the mean livelihood he could draw from more praiseworthy pursuits in the Norwegian fjords. The accident of his country lying at the trans-Baltic end of the great trans-Continental trade-route had provided him with the knowledge of making steel weapons in great number and abundance. Raiding Scotland, he was in no sense a superior or heroic type subduing a lowly or inferior; he was merely a pirate with a good cutlass, a thug with a sudden and efficient strangling-rope. Yet those dull, dyspeptic whey-faced clowns have figured in all orthodox histories as the bringers of something new and vital to Scottish culture, as an invigorating strain, a hard and splendid ingredient. If is farcical that it should be necessary to affirm at this late day that the Norseman brought nothing of any permanence to Scotland other than his characteristic gastritis.

Yet that cutlass carved great sections from the Scottish coasts: presently all the Western Isles had suffered a profound infiltration of the thin, mean blood of the northern sea-raiders. In the east, the attacks were almost purely burglarious. The hardy Norseman, with his long grey face so unfortunately reminiscent of a horse's, would descend on that and this village or township, steal and rape and fire, and then race for his ships to escape encounter with the local levies. On such occasions as he landed in any force, and met the Picts (even the idiotically badly-led, Kelt-led Picts) in any force, he would, as at the Battle of Aberlemno, be routed with decision and vigour. Yet those constant raidings weakened the Eastern kingdom of the Picts: in A.D. 844 the Scot king, Kenneth MacAlpin, succeeded to the Pictish throne – it was evidently regarded as the succession of a superior to the estates of an inferior. Thereafter the name Pict disappears from Scottish history, though, paradoxically immortal, the Pict remained.

From 1034, when Duncan ascended the Scottish throne, until 1603, when James VI ascended the English throne,

Scotland occupied herself, willy-nilly, in upbuilding her second (and last) characteristic civilization. Her first, as we have seen, was that modification of the Archaic Civilization which the Kelts overthrew; this second which slowly struggled into being under the arrow-hails, the ridings and rapings and throat-cuttings of official policy, the jealous restraints of clerical officialdom, was compounded of many cultural strands. It was in essentials a Pictish civilization, as the vast majority of the inhabitants remained Picts. But, in the Lowlands, it had changed once again its speech, relinquishing the alien Keltic in favour of the equally alien Anglo-Saxon. The exchange was a matter of domestic policy, a febrific historical accident hinged on the bed-favours wrung from his consort by the henpecked Malcolm Canmore.

The third of the name of Malcolm to rule in Scotland, his speech, his court, and his official pronunciamentos were all Keltic until he wedded the Princess Margaret, who had fled from the Norman invasion of England. A greatniece of Edward the Confessor, Margaret was a pious daughter of the Church and greatly shocked at the Keltic deviations from Roman dates and ceremonial incantations. She devoted her life to bringing the usages of the Scottish Church into harmony with orthodox Catholicism. She bred assiduously: she bred six sons and two daughters, and in return for the delights of the shameful intimacies which begat this offspring, the abashed Malcolm refrained from any hand in their christening. They were all christened with good English names, they were taught English as their native speech, they lived to grow up and Anglicize court and church and town. Of the two great women in Scots history it is doubtful if the most calamitously pathological influence should be ascribed to Margaret the Good or to Mary the Unchaste.

Yet this Anglicization was a surface Anglicization. English speech and English culture alike were as yet fluid things: it meant no cultural subjection to the southern half of the island. It begat a tradition, a speech, an art and a literature in the southern half of Scotland which were set in an Anglo-Saxon, not an English, mould, but filled with the deep spiritual awarenesses of the great basic race which wielded this new cultural weapon as once it had wielded the Keltic. It was a thing national and with a homely and accustomed feel, this language in which Wyntoun and Barbour and Blind Harry were presently telling the epic stories of the great War of Independence.

The effect of that war, the unceasing war of several centuries, was calamitous to the Scots civilization in the sense that it permanently impoverished it, leaving Scotland, but for a brief blink, always a poor country economically, and a blessing in that it set firmly in the Scots mind the knowledge of national homogeneity: Scotland was the home of true political nation-alism (once a liberating influence, not as now an inhibiting one) – not the nationalism forced upon an unwilling or in-different people by the intrigues of kings and courtesans, but the spontaneous up-rising of an awareness of blood-brotherhood and freedom-right. In the midst of the many dreary and shameful pages of the book of Scottish history the story of the rising of the Scots under the leadership of William Wallace still rings splendid and amazing. Wallace was one of the few authentic national heroes: authentic in the sense that he apprehended and moulded the historic forces of his time in a fashion denied to all but a few of the world's great political leaders – Cromwell, Lincoln, Lenin.

It was 1296. Scotland, after a dynastic squabble on the rights of this and that boorish noble to ascend the Scottish throne and there cheat and fornicate after the divine rights of kings, had been conquered, dismembered and ground in the mud by Edward the First of England. He did it with a cold and bored efficiency, as a man chastising and chaining a slobbering, yelping cur. Then he returned to England; and the chained cur suddenly awoke in the likeness of a lion.

'The instinct of the Scottish people,' wrote John Richard Green, 'has guided it right in choosing Wallace for its national hero. He was the first to assert freedom as a national birthright.' His assertion roused Scotland. The peasants flocked to his standard – suddenly, and for perhaps the first time in Scots history, stirred beyond their customary indifference over the quarrels of their rulers. Here was something new, a leader who promised something new. Nor did he only promise: presently he was accomplishing. At the head of a force that bore the significant title of the 'Army of the Commons of Scotland' Wallace met and routed the English in pitched battle at Cambuskenneth Bridge in 1297, was offered the crown of Scotland, refused it, and instead was nominated Guardian of Scotland, a great republican with the first of the great republican titles, albeit he called himself a royalist.

For a year it seemed his cause would sweep everything before it. The laggard nobles came to join him. Presently the Army of the Commons of Scotland was being poisoned by the usual aristocratic intrigues, though still the troubled peasants and townsmen clung to their faith in the Guardian. Then news came that Edward in person was on the march against Scotland. Wallace assembled all his forces and met the invader at Falkirk. The Scots cavalry, noble-recruited, noble-led, strategically placed to fall on the ranks of the English archers and rout them at the crucial moment, fled without striking a blow. Wallace's great schiltrouns of heroic peasant spearmen were broken and dispersed.

Wallace himself sailed for France, seeking aid there for his distracted country. In 1304 he returned, was captured by the English, tried and condemned as a traitor, and hanged, castrated, and disembowelled on Tower Hill. This judicial murder is one of the first and most dreadful examples of that characteristic English frightfulness wielded throughout history against the defenders of alien and weaker peoples. More serious than Wallace's personal fate, it murdered that fine hope and enthusiasm that had stirred the Army of the Scots Commons on the morning of Falkirk. In a kind of despairing hatred, not hope, the Scots people turned to support the rebellions of the various shoddy noble adventurers who now raised the standard against the English. By intrigue, assassination, and some strategical skill one of those nobles, Robert the Brus, had presently disposed of all his rivals, had himself crowned king, and, after various reverses and flights and hidings and romantic escapades in company with spiders and Lorne loons, succeeded in routing the English at the Battle of Bannockburn. With that victory the Scots royalties came to their own again, however little the Scots commons.

Yet, in the succeeding centuries of wars and raids, dynastic begettings and dynastic blood-lettings, the commons of Scotland showed a vigour both un-English and un-French in defence of the rights of the individual. Villeinage died early in Scotland: the independent tenant-retainer came early on the scene in the Lowlands. In the Highlands the clan system, ostensibly aristocratic, was never so in actuality. It was a communistic patriarchy, the relation of the chief to his meanest clansman the relation of an elder blood brother, seldom of a noble to a serf. The guildsmen of the towns modelled their policies on those of the Hansa cities and Augsburg, rather than on the slavish subservience of their contemporaries in England. Presently the French alliance, disastrous from a military point of view, was profoundly leavening the character of Scots culture, leavening, not obliterating it. Scots built and carved and sang and wrote with new tools of technique and vocabulary to hand. The Scots civilization of the fifteenth and sixteenth centuries absorbed its great cultural impulses from the Continent; as a consequence, Scots literature in the fifteenth century is already a great literature while in contemporary England there is little more than the maundering of a poetasting host of semi-illiterates. Despite the feuds and squabbles of noble and king, there came into being a rude plenty in Scotland of the fifteenth and sixteenth centuries. The reign of James the Fourth was, economically and culturally, the Golden Age of the great Scots civilization. Its duration was brief and its fate soon that which had overtaken the Golden Age of the happy Pict hunters three thousand years before.

The end of James the Fourth at Flodden in 1513, the dark end to the greatest raid of the Scots into England, plunged the country into fifteen years of mis-government, when this and that clownish noble attempted to seize the power through this and that intrigue of palace and bedchamber. The Golden Age faded rapidly as marauding bands of horse clattered up the cobbled streets of the towns and across the fertile Lowland crop-lands. By the time the Fifth James assumed the power Scotland was a distracted country, the commons bitterly taxed and raided and oppressed, the ruler in castle and keep a gorged and stinking carrion-crow. James, the Commons' King, the one heroic royalty in Scots history, faced a hopeless task with the broken and impoverished commons but half aware of his championship. He put down the nobles with a ruthless hand, defied the monk-murdering Henry VIII of England, established the Court of Session and the Supreme Court of Justice; he might well have re-established the economic prosperity of his father's reign but for the English invasion of the country in 1542. The nobles refused to join the army he raised – the pitiful Church army routed at Solway Moss. Dying at Falkland Palace a few days later James, God's Scotsman as he has been well called, heard of the birth of a daughter. 'It cam wi' a lass and 'twill gang wi' a lass,' he said, speaking perhaps of his own dynasty; unforeseeing the fact that it was the Scots civilization itself that that daughter was to see in early eclipse.

That eclipse was inaugurated by the coming of the tumultuous change in Christian ritualism and superstitious practice dignified by the name of Reformation. Into its many causes in Western Europe there is no need to enter here. Nobles hungered to devour Church lands; churchmen were often then, as later, cowardly and avaricious souls; the Church, then as often, seemed intellectually moribund, a dead weight lying athwart the minds of men. So, in apparent dispute as to the correct method of devouring the symbolic body of the dead god, symbolically slain, hell was let loose on the European scene for a long two hundred years. Men fought and died with

enthusiasm in the cause of ceremonial cannibalism. In Scotland
the Reforming party had been growing to power even in the
age of the Fifth James. During the long minority of his daughter,
Mary Queen of Scots, it was frequently in possession of the
reins of power: in 1557 it gathered together its forces and
signed a National Convention for the establishment of the
Reformed Faith.

Two years afterwards the ecclesiastic, John Knox, returned
from a long exile in England and on the Continent. Knox had
served as a slave on the French galleys for eighteen months
after the assassination of Cardinal Beaton in 1546, he had
definite and clear beliefs on the part the Reformation must
play in Scotland, and in the years of his exile he had wandered
from haunt to haunt of the European revolutionaries (much
as Lenin did in the first decade of the twentieth century)
testing out his own creed in converse and debate with Calvin
and the like innovators. Once again a Scotsman had arisen
capable of apprehending the direction of the historic forces,
and determined to enchannel those for the benefit of a Commons' Scotland. The nauseous character of his political allies
in Scotland did not deter him from the conflict. In the triumphant Parliament summoned in 1560 the Protestants under
his direction established the Reformed Church, forbade the
mass, and practically legalized the wholesale seizure of Church
property. Knox's intentions with regard to the disposal of
that property were definite and unshakable: it would be used
for the relief of the poor, for the establishment of free schools,
for the sustentation of a free people's priesthood. But, though
he had foreseen the direction of the historic forces thus far,
history proved on the side of his robbing allies, not on his.
The Covenant left the Commons poorer than ever and Knox
an embittered and sterile leader, turning from his battle in
the cause of the people to sardonic denunciations of the minor
moral lapses of the young Queen.

He was a leader defeated: and history was to ascribe to him
and his immediate followers, and with justice, blame for some

of the most terrible aberrations of the Scots spirit in succeeding centuries. Yet Knox himself was of truly heroic mould; had his followers, far less his allies, been of like mettle, the history of Scotland might have been strangely and splendidly different. To pose him against the screen of antique time as an inhibition-ridden neurotic (as is the modern fashion) who murdered the spirit and hope of an heroic young queen, is malicious distortion of the true picture. The 'heroic young queen' in question had the face, mind, manners and morals of a well-intentioned but hysterical poodle.

Her succession by the calamitous Sixth James, who was summoned to the English throne in 1603, was the beginning of the end of the Scots civilization. That end came quickly. Not only had temporal power moved from Edinburgh to London (for at least a while) but the cultural focus had shifted as well. There began that long process of barbarization of the Scots mind and culture which is still in progress. Presently it was understood to be rather a shameful thing to be a Scotsman, to make Scots poetry, to be subject to Scots law, to be an inhabitant of the northern half of the island. The Diffusionist school of historians holds that the state of Barbarism is no half-way house of a progressive people towards full and complete civilization: on the contrary, it marks a degeneration from an older civilization, as Savagery is the state of a people absorbing only the poorer elements of an alien culture. The state of Scotland since the Union of the Crowns gives remarkable support to this view, though the savagery of large portions of the modern urbanized population had a fresh calamity – the Industrial Revolution – to father it.

Yet, though all art is no more than the fine savour and essence of the free life, its decay and death in Scotland was no real mark of the subjection and decay of the free Scottish spirit: it was merely a mark of that spirit in an anguished travail that has not yet ceased. Presently, gathering that unquenchable force into new focus, came the Covenanting Times, the call of the Church of Knox to be defended as the

74

Church of the Commons, of the People, bitterly assailed by noble and King. That the call was justified we may doubt, that the higher councils of the Church government themselves were other than sedulously manipulated tyrannies in the hands of the old landed Keltic gentry may also be doubted. But to large sections of the Lowland Scots the Covenant was not so much a sworn bond between themselves and God as between their own souls and freedom. They flocked to its standards in the second Bishops' War, they invaded England. For a time the Covenanting Scots Army at Newcastle dictated English policy, ruled England, and almost imposed on it the Presbytery. Thereafter, in the sway and clash of the Parliamentarian wars, it suffered collapse under the weight of its own prosperity and rottenness. Cromwell forcibly dissolved the General Assembly of the Scots Church in 1653, incorporated Scotland in the Commonwealth, and marched home leaving a country under English military governance – a country chastised and corrected, but strangely unbroken in spirit. Scotland and the Scots, after a gasp of surprise, accepted Cromwell with a wary trust. Here, and again, as once in those brief days when the standards of the Guardian of Scotland unfurled by Stirling Brig, was something new on the Scottish scene – English-inspired, but new and promising. If they laboured under dictatorship, so did the English. If their nobles were proscribed and persecuted, so were the English. If their frontier was down, trade with England and the English colonies was free. . . . It was a glimpse of the Greater Republicanism; and it faded almost before Scotland could look on it. The Second Charles returned and enforced the Episcopacy on the Scots, and from 1660 until 1690 Scotland travailed in such political Terror as has few parallels in history.

The People's Church gathered around it the peasants – especially the western peasants – in its defence. At Rullion Green the Covenanting Army was defeated, and an orgy of suppression followed. Covenanters were tortured with rigour and a sadistic ingenuity before being executed in front of

their own houses, in sight of their own women-folk. In the
forefront of this business of oppression were the Scots nobles,
led by Graham of Claverhouse, 'Bonny Dundee'. This remarkable individual, so much biographïed and romanticized by
later generations, was both a sadist and a criminal degenerate.
He was one in a long train of the Scots nobility. He had few
qualities to recommend him, his generalship was poor and his
strategy worse. Torturing unarmed peasants was the utmost
reach of statesmanship ever achieved by this hero of the
romantics. Where he met an army – even a badly organized
army as at Drumclog – he was ignominiously defeated and
fled with the speed and panic of the thin-blooded pervert
that he was. His last battle, that of Killiecrankie, he won by
enlisting the aid of the Highlanders against those whom they
imagined to be their enemies. His portrayed face has a rat-
like look in the mean, cold eyes; his name has a sour stench
still in the pages of Scottish history.

That last battle of his marked almost the end of the Church
persecutions: the Kirk of Scotland emerged with the Revolution from its long night into a day of power and pomp. So
doing, following an infallible law of history, it shed the
enthusiasm and high loyalty of all generous souls. From 1690
onwards the history of the churches in Scotland is a history
of minor and unimportant brawling on questions of state
support and state denunciation, it is an oddly political history,
reflecting the dreary play of politics up to and after the Union
of the Parliaments, the Union which destroyed the last out-
ward symbols of the national civilization.

Whatever the growing modern support for repudiation of
that Union, it is well to realize that the first tentative moves
towards it came from the side of the Scots Parliament, if not
of the Scots people. As early as 1689 the Scots Parliament
appointed commissioners to treat for an 'incorporating union',
though nothing came of it. Scottish trade and Scottish industry
was very desperately hampered by the English Navigation
Act, in which Scots were treated as aliens; and also by the

fact that the Scots lacked any overseas dominion on which to dump their surpluses of wealth and population – though indeed, except in the farcical economics of that time (ours are no less farcical) they had surpluses of neither. The first attempts at Union came to nothing: the Scots turned their energies to founding a colony in Darien.

The attempt was disastrous: the Spaniards, already in possession, and aided and abetted by powerful English influences, beat off the settlers. News of the disaster killed among the Scots people any desire for union with the auld enemy; nor indeed did they ever again support it. The Union was brought about by as strange a series of intrigues as history is aware of: England ingeniously bribed her way to power. There was little real resistance in the Scots Parliament except by such lonely figures as Fletcher of Saltoun. On May 1st, 1707, Scotland officially ceased to be a country and became 'that part of the United Kingdom, North Britain.' Scotsmen officially ceased to be Scots, and became Britons – presumably North Britons. England similarly lost identity – impatiently, on a scrap of paper. But everyone knew, both at home and abroad, that what really had happened was the final subjugation of the Scots by the English, and the absorption of the northern people into the polity and name of the southern.

There was a smouldering fire of resistance: it sprang to flame twice in the course of the first half-century. In 1715 the Earl of Mar raised the standard for the exiled Jacobite King. He received a support entirely unwarranted by either his own person or that of the puppet monarch whose cause he championed. At the strange, drawn battle of Sheriffmuir the Jacobite rebellion was not so much suppressed as suddenly bored. It was as though its supporters were overtaken by a desire to yawn at the whole affair. They melted from the field, not to assemble, they or their sons, for another thirty years.

This was with the landing of Prince Charles Edward in the Highlands in 1745. Scotland – Scotland of the Highlands, great sections of Scotland of the Lowlands – took him to her heart. The clans rose in his support, not unwillingly following the call of their chiefs. Here was relief from that crushing sense of inferiority that had pressed on the nation since the first day of the Union: here was one who promised to restore the Ancient Times – the time of meal and milk and plenty of the Fifth James; here was one who promised Scotland her nationhood again. In after years it became the fashion to pretend that the vast mass of the Scots people were indifferent to, or hostile to, this last adventure of the Stewarts. But there was no Scotsman worthy of the name who was not, at least at first, an enthusiast and a partisan.

Charles marched from victory to victory: presently he was marching across the Borders with an ill-equipped army of Highlanders and Lowland levies, seeking the support promised him by the English Jacobites. He sought it in vain. To the English Jacobite, to all the English, it was plain that here was no exiled English king come to reclaim his throne: here was something long familiar in wars with the northern enemy – a Scots army on a raid. Charles turned back at Derby, and, turning, lost the campaign, lost the last chance to restore the ancient nationhood of Scotland, lost (which was of no importance) himself.

His final defeat at Culloden inaugurated the ruthless extirpation of the clan system in the Highlands, the extirpation of almost a whole people. Sheep-farming came to the Highlands, depopulating its glens, just as the Industrial Revolution was coming to the Lowlands, enriching the new plutocracy and brutalizing the ancient plebs. Glasgow and Greenock were coming into being as the last embers of the old Scots culture flickered and fuffed and went out.

There followed that century and a half which leads us to the present day, a century through which we hear the wail of children in unending factories and in night-time slums, the rantings of place-seeking politicians, the odd chirping and cackling of the bastardized Scots romantic schools in music and literature. It is a hundred and fifty years of unloveliness and pridelessness, of growing wealth and growing impoverishment, of Scotland sharing in the rise and final torturing maladjustments of that economic system which holds all the modern world in thrall. It was a hundred and fifty years in which the ancient Pictish spirit remembered only at dim intervals, as in a nightmare, the cry of the wind in the hair of freemen in that ancient life of the Golden Age, the play of the same wind in the banners of Wallace when he marshalled his schiltrouns at Falkirk.

GLASGOW

Glasgow is one of the few places in Scotland which defy personification. To image Edinburgh as a disappointed spinster, with a hare-lip and inhibitions, is at least to approximate as closely to the truth as to image the Prime Mover as a Levantine Semite. So with Dundee, a frowsy fisher-wife addicted to gin and infanticide, Aberdeen a thin-lipped peasant-woman who has borne eleven and buried nine. But no Scottish image of personification may display, even distortedly, the essential Glasgow. One might go further afield, to the tortured imaginings of the Asiatic mind, to find her likeness – many-armed Siva with the waistlet of skulls, or Xipe of Ancient America, whose priest skinned the victim alive, and then clad himself in the victim's skin. . . . But one doubts anthropomorphic representation at all. The monster of Loch Ness is probably the lost soul of Glasgow, in scales and horns, disporting itself in the Highlands after evacuating finally and completely its mother-corpse.

One cannot blame it. My distant cousin, Mr. Leslie Mitchell, once described Glasgow in one of his novels as 'the vomit of a cataleptic commercialism'. But it is more than that. It may be a corpse, but the maggot-swarm upon it is very fiercely alive. One cannot watch and hear the long beat of traffic down Sauchiehall, or see its eddy and spume where St. Vincent Street and Renfield Street cross, without realizing what excellent grounds the old-fashioned anthropologist appeared to have for believing that man was by nature a brutish savage, a herd-beast delighting in vocal discordance and orgiastic aural abandon.

Loch Lomond lies quite near to Glasgow. Nice Glaswegians motor out there and admire the scenery and calculate its horse-power and drink whisky and chaff one another in genteelly Anglicized Glaswegianisms. After a hasty look at Glasgow the investigator would do well to disguise himself as one of like kind, drive down to Loch Lomondside and stare across its waters at the sailing clouds that crown the Ben, at the flooding of colours changing and darkling and miraculously lighting up and down those misty slopes, where night comes over long mountain leagues that know only the paddings of the shy, stray hare, the whirr and cry of the startled pheasant, silences so deep you can hear the moon come up, mornings so greyly coloured they seem stolen from Norse myth. This is the proper land and stance from which to look at Glasgow, to divest oneself of horror or shame or admiration or – very real – fear, and ask: Why? Why did men ever allow themselves to become enslaved to a thing so obscene and so foul when there was *this* awaiting them here – hills and the splendours of freedom and silence, the clean splendours of hunger and woe and dread in the winds and rains and famine-times of the earth, hunting and love and the call of the moon? Nothing endured by the primitives who once roamed those hills – nothing of woe or terror – approximated in degree or kind to that life that festers in the courts and wynds and alleys of Camlachie, Govan, the Gorbals.

In Glasgow there are over a hundred and fifty thousand human beings living in such conditions as the most bitterly pressed primitive in Tierra del Fuego never visioned. They live five or six to the single room. . . . And at this point, sitting and staring at Ben Lomond, it requires a vivid mental jerk to realize the quality of that room. It is not a room in a large and airy building; it is not a single-roomed hut on the verge of a hill; it is not a cave driven into free rock, in the sound of the sea-birds, as that old Azilian cave in Argyll: it is a room that is part of some great sloven of tenement – the tenement itself in a line or a grouping with hundreds of its fellows, its windows grimed with the unceasing wash and drift of coal-dust, its stairs narrow and befouled and steep, its evening breath like that which might issue from the mouth of a lung-diseased beast. The hundred and fifty thousand eat and sleep and copulate and conceive and crawl into childhood in those waste jungles of stench and disease and hopelessness, sub-humans as definitely as the Morlocks of Wells – and without even the consolation of feeding on their oppressors' flesh.

A hundred and fifty thousand . . . and all very like you or me or my investigator sitting appalled on the banks of Loch Lomond (where he and his true love will never meet again). And they live on food of the quality of offal, ill-cooked, ill-eaten with speedily-diseased teeth for the tending of which they can afford no fees; they work – if they have work – in factories or foundries or the roaring reek of the Docks toilsome and dreary and unimaginative hours – hour on hour, day on day, frittering away the tissues of their bodies and the spirit-stuff of their souls; they are workless – great numbers of them – doomed to long days of staring vacuity, of shoelessness, of shivering hidings in this and that mean runway when the landlords' agents come, of mean and desperate beggings at Labour Exchanges and Public Assistance Committees; their voices are the voices of men and women robbed of manhood and womanhood. . . .

The investigator on Loch Lomondside shudders and turns to culture for comfort. He is, of course, a subscriber to *The Modern Scot,* where culture at three removes – castrated, disembowelled, and genteelly vulgarized – is served afresh each season; and has brought his copy with him. Mr. Adam Kennedy is serializing a novel, *The Mourners,* his technique a genteel objectivity. And one of his characters has stopped in Glasgow's Kelvingrove, and is savouring its essence:

'John's eyes savoured the spaciousness of the crescent, the formal curve of the unbroken line of house facades, the regimentation of the rows of chimney-pots, the full-length windows, the unnecessarily broad front steps, the feudal basements – savoured all these in the shimmering heat of the day just as his nose had savoured the morning freshness. It was as good for him to walk round these old terraces as to visit a cathedral. He could imagine now and then that he had evoked for himself something of the atmosphere of the grand days of these streets. The world was surer of itself then, sure of the ultimate perfectability of man, sure of the ultimate mastery over the forces that surrounded him. And if Atlas then no longer had the world firm on his shoulder, the world for all that rested on the same basis of the thus-and-thusness of things. With such a basis you could have that sureness of yourself to do things largely as had been done before. But the modern mind was no longer sure of itself even in a four-roomed bungalow. Its pride was the splitting of its personality into broods of impish devils that spent their time spying one on the other. It could never get properly outside itself, could never achieve the objectivity that was capable of such grandly deliberate planning as in these streets.'

Glasgow speaks. The hundred and fifty thousand are answered. Glasgow has spoken.

This, indeed, is its attitude, not merely the pale whey of intellectualism peculiar to *The Modern Scot*. The bourgeois Glaswegian cultivates æsthetic objectivity as happier men cultivate beards or gardens. Pleasant folk of Kelvingrove point out that those hundred and fifty thousand – how well off they are! Free education, low rents, no rates, State relief – half of them, in fact, State pensioners. Besides, they enjoy life as they are – damn them, or they ought to. Always raising riots about their conditions. Not that they raise the riots themselves – it's the work of the communists – paid agitators from Moscow. But they've long since lost all hold. Or they ought to have——

In those days of Nationalism, of Douglasism, (that ingenious scheme for childbirth without pain and – even more intriguing – without a child), of Socialism, of Fascism, Glasgow, as no other place, moves me to a statement of faith. I have amused myself with many political creeds – the more egregrious the

creed the better. I like the thought of a Scots Republic with
Scots Border Guards in saffron kilts – the thought of those
kilts can awake me to joy in the middle of the night. I like the
thought of Miss Wendy Wood leading a Scots Expeditionary
Force down to Westminster to reclaim the Scone Stone:
I would certainly march with that expedition myself in spite
of the risk of dying of laughter by the way. I like the thought
of a Scots Catholic kingdom with Mr. Compton Mackenzie
Prime Minister to some disinterred Jacobite royalty, and all
the Scots intellectuals settled out on the land on thirty-acre
crofts, or sent to recolonize St. Kilda for the good of their
souls and the nation (except the hundreds streaming over the
Border in panic flight at sight of this Scotland of their dreams).
I like the thought of the ancient Scots aristocracy revived and
set in order by Mr. George Blake, that ephor of the people:
Mr. Blake vetoing the Duke of Montrose is one of my dearest
visions. I like the thoughts of the Scottish Fascists evicting all
those of Irish blood from Scotland, and so leaving Albyn
entirely deserted but for some half-dozen pro-Irish Picts like
myself. I like the thought of a Scottish Socialist Republic
under Mr. Maxton – preferably at war with royalist England,
and Mr. Maxton summoning the Russian Red Army to his
aid (the Red Army digging a secret tunnel from Archangel
to Aberdeen). And I like the thought of Mr. R. M. Black and
his mysterious Free Scots, that modern Mafia, assassinating
the Bankers (which is what bankers are for). . . .

But I cannot play with those fantasies when I think of the
hundred and fifty thousand in Glasgow. They are a something
that stills the parlour chatter. I find I am by way of being
an intellectual myself. I meet and talk with many people
whose interests are art and letters and music, enthusiasm for
this and that aspect of craft and architecture, men and women
who have very warm and sincere beliefs indeed regarding the
ancient culture of Scotland, people to whom Glasgow is the
Hunterian Museum with its fine array of Roman coins, or
the Galleries with their equally fine array of pictures. 'Culture'

is the motif-word of the conversation: ancient Scots culture, future Scots culture, culture ad lib. and ad nauseam. . . . The patter is as intimate on my tongue as on theirs. And relevant to the fate and being of those hundred and fifty thousand it is no more than the chatter and scratch of a band of apes, seated in a pit on a midden of corpses.

There is nothing in culture or art that is worth the life and elementary happiness of one of those thousands who rot in the Glasgow slums. There is nothing in science or religion. If it came (as it may come) to some fantastic choice between a free and independent Scotland, a centre of culture, a bright flame of artistic and scientific achievement, and providing elementary decencies of food and shelter to the submerged proletariat of Glasgow and Scotland, I at least would have no doubt as to which side of the battle I would range myself. For the cleansing of that horror, if cleanse it they could, I would welcome the English in suzerainty over Scotland till the end of time. I would welcome the end of Braid Scots and Gaelic, our culture, our history, our nationhood under the heels of a Chinese army of occupation if it could cleanse the Glasgow slums, give a surety of food and play – the elementary right of every human being – to those people of the abyss. . . . .

I realize (seated on the plump modernity of *The Modern Scot* by the side of my investigator out on Loch Lomond-bank) how completely I am the complete Philistine. I have always liked the Philistines, a commendable and gracious and cleanly race. They built clean cities with wide, airy streets, they delighted in the singing of good, simple songs and hunting and lovemaking and the worshipping of relevant and comprè-hensible Gods. They were a light in the Ancient East and led simple and happy and carefree lives, with a splendour of trumpets now and again to stir them to amusing orgy. . . . And above, in the hills, in Jerusalem, dwelt the Israelites, unwashed and unashamed, horrified at the clean anarchy which is the essence of life, oppressed by grisly fears of life and death and time, suborning simple human pleasures in living into an insane debating on justice and right, the Good Life, the Soul of Man, artistic canon, the First Cause, National Ethos, the mainsprings of conduct, æsthetic approach – and all the rest of the dirty little toys with which dirty little men in dirty little caves love to play, turning with a haughty shudder of repulsion from the cry of the wind and the beat of the sun on the hills outside. . . . One of the greatest tragedies of the ancient world was the killing of Goliath by David – a ghoul-haunted little village squirt who sneaked up and murdered the Philistine while the latter (with a good breakfast below his belt) was admiring the sunrise.

The non-Philistines never admire sunrises. They never admire good breakfasts. Their ideal is the half-starved at sunset, whose actions and appearances they can record with a proper æsthetic detachment. One of the best-loved pictures of an earlier generation of Glasgow intellectuals was Josef Israel's *Frugal Meal* in the Glasgow Galleries. Even yet the modern will halt you to admire the chiaroscuro, the fine shades and attitudes. But you realize he is a liar. He is merely an inhibited little sadist, and his concentrated essence of enjoyment is the hunger and dirt and hopelessness of the two figures in question. He calls this a 'robust acceptance of life'.

Sometime, it is true, the non-Philistine of past days had a qualm of regret, a notion, a thin pale abortion of an idea that life in simplicity was life in essence. So he painted a man or a woman, nude only in the less shameful portions of his or her anatomy (egregious bushes were called in to hide the genital shames) and called it not *Walking* or *Running* or *Staring* or *Sleeping* or *Lusting* (as it generally was) but *Light* or *Realization* or *The Choir* or what not. A Millais in the Glasgow Galleries is an excellent example, which neither you nor my investigator may miss. It is the non-Philistine's wistful idea of (in capitals) Life in Simplicity – a decent young childe in a breech-clout about to play hoop-la with a forked stick. But instead of labelling this truthfully and obviously *Portrait of Shy-Making Intellectual Playing at Boy Scouts* it is called (of course) *The Forerunner*.

The bourgeois returns at evening these days to Kelvingrove, to Woodsidehill, to Hillhead and Dowanhill with heavy and doubting steps. The shipyards are still, with rusting cranes and unbefouled waters nearby, in Springburn the empty factories increase and multiply, there are dead windows and barred factory-gates in Bridgeton and Mile End. Commercialism has returned to its own vomit too often and too long still to find sustenance therein. Determinedly in Glasgow (as elsewhere) they call this condition 'The Crisis', and, in the fashion of a Christian Scientist whose actual need is cascara, invoke Optimism for its cure. But here as nowhere else in the modern world of capitalism does the impartial investigator realize that the remedy lies neither in medicine nor massage, but in surgery. . . . The doctors (he hears) are gathered for the Saturday-Sunday diagnoses on Glasgow Green; and betakes himself there accordingly.

But there (as elsewhere) the physicians disagree – multitudes of physicians, surrounded by anxious groups of the ailing patient's dependents. A brief round of the various physicians convinces the investigator of one thing: the unpopularity of surgery. The single surgeon orating is, of course, the Communist. His gathering is small. A larger following attends Mr. Guy Aldred, Non-Parliamentary Anarchocommunist, pledged to use neither knives nor pills, but invocation of the Gospels according to St. Bakunin. Orthodox Socialism, ruddy and plump, with the spoils from the latest Glasgow Corporation swindle in its pocket, the fee'd physician, popular and pawky, is fervent and optimistic. Pills? – Nonsense! Surgery? – Muscovite savagery! What is needed to remove the sprouting pustules from the fair face of commercialism is merely a light, non-greasy ointment (which will not stain the sheets). Near at hand stands the Fascist: the investigator, with a training which has hitherto led him to debar the Neanderthaler from the direct ancestral line of *Homo Sapiens,* stares at this ethnological note of interrogation. The Fascist diagnosis: Lack of blood. Remedy: Bleeding. A Nationalist holds forth near by.

What the patient needs is not more food, fresh air, a decent
room of his own and a decent soul of his own – No! What he
needs is the air he ceased to breathe two hundred and fifty
years ago – specially reclaimed and canned by the National
Part of Scotland (and forwarded in plain vans.) ... A
Separatist casts scorn on the Nationalist's case. What the
patient requires is: Separation. Separation from England,
from English speech, English manners, English food, English
clothes, English culinary and English common sense. Then
he will recover.

It is coming on dark, as they say in the Scotland that is
not Glasgow. And out of the Gorbals arises again that foul
breath as of a dying beast.

You turn from Glasgow Green with a determination to
inspect this Gorbals on your own. It is incredibly un-Scottish.
It is lovably and abominably and delightfully and hideously
un-Scottish. It is not even a Scottish slum. Stout men in beards
and ringlets and unseemly attire lounge and strut with pointed
shoes: Ruth and Naomi go by with downcast Eastern faces,
the Lascar rubs shoulder with the Syrian, Harry Lauder is a
Baal unkeened to the midnight stars. In the air the stench is
of a different quality to Govan's or Camlachie's, – a better
quality. It is not filth and futility and boredom unrelieved.
It is haunted by an ancient ghost of goodness and grossness,
sun-warmed and ripened under alien suns. It is the most
saving slum in Glasgow, and the most abandoned. Emerging
from it, the investigator suddenly realizes why he sought it in
such haste from Glasgow Green: it was in order that he might
assure himself there were really and actually other races on
the earth apart from the Scots!

So long I have wanted to write what I am about to write –
but hitherto I have lacked the excuse. Glasgow provides it. ...
About Nationalism. About Small Nations. What a curse to
the earth are small nations! Latvia, Lithuania, Poland, Finland,
San Salvador, Luxembourg, Manchukuo, the Irish Free State.
There are many more: there is an appalling number of dis-

gusting little stretches of the globe claimed, occupied and infected by groupings of babbling little morons – babbling militant on the subjects (unendingly) of their *exclusive* cultures, their *exclusive* languages, their *national* souls, their *national* genius, their unique achievements in throat-cutting in this and that abominable little squabble in the past. Mangy little curs a-yap above their minute hoardings of shrivelled bones, they cease from their yelpings at the passers-by only in such intervals as they devote to civil-war flea-hunts. Of all the accursed progeny of World War, surely the worst was this dwarf mongrel-litter. The South Irish of the middle class were never pleasant persons: since they obtained their Free State the belch of their pride in the accents of their unhygienic patois has given the unfortunate Irish Channel the seeming of a cess-pool. Having blamed their misfortunes on England for centuries, they achieved independence and promptly found themselves incapable of securing that independence by the obvious and necessary operation – social revolution. Instead: revival of Gaelic, bewildering an unhappy world with uncouth spellings and titles and postage-stamps; revival of the blood feud; revival of the decayed literary cultus which (like most products of the Kelt) was an abomination even while actually alive and but poor manure when it died. . . . Or Finland – Communist-murdering Finland – ruled by German Generals and the Central European foundries, boasting to its ragged population the return of its ancient literary culture like a senile octogenarian boasting the coming of second childhood. . . . And we are bidden go and do likewise:

'For we are not opposed to English influence only at those points where it expresses itself in political domination and financial and economic over-control, but we are (or ought to be) opposed to English influence at all points. Not only must English governmental control be overthrown, but the English language must go, and English methods of education, English fashions in dress, English models in the arts, English ideals, everything English. Everything English must go.'

This is a Mr. Ludovic Grant, writing in *The Free Man*. Note what the Scot is bidden to give up: the English language, that lovely and flexible instrument, so akin to the darker Braid Scots which has been the Scotsman's tool of thought for a thousand years. English methods of education: which are derived from Germano-French-Italian models. English fashions in dress: invented in Paris – London – Edinburgh – Timbuktu – Calcutta – Chichen-Itza – New York. English models in the arts: nude models as well, no doubt – Scots models in future must sprout three pairs of arms and a navel in the likeness of a lion rampant. English ideals: decency, freedom, justice, ideals innate in the mind of man, as common to the Bantu as to the Kentishman – those also he must relinquish. . . . It will profit Glasgow's hundred and fifty thousand slumdwellers so much to know that they are being starved and brutalized by Labour Exchanges and Public Assistance Committees staffed exclusively by Gaelic-speaking, haggis-eating Scots in saffron kilts and tongued brogues, full of such typical Scottish ideals as those which kept men chained as slaves in the Fifeshire mines a century or so ago. . . .

Glasgow's salvation, Scotland's salvation, the world's salvation lies in neither nationalism nor internationalism, those twin halves of an idiot whole. It lies in ultimate cosmopolitanism, the earth the City of God, the Brahmaputra and Easter Island as free and familiar to the man from Govan as the Molendinar and Bute. A time will come when the self-wrought, prideful differentiations of Scotsman, Englishman, Frenchman, Spaniard will seem as ludicrous as the infantile squabblings of the Heptarchians. A time will come when nationalism, with other cultural aberrations, will have passed from the human spirit, when Man, again free and unchained, has all the earth for his footstool, sings his epics in a language moulded from the best on earth, draws his heroes, his sunrises, his valleys

and his mountains from all the crinkles of our lovely planet. . . .
And we are bidden to abandon this vision for the delights of
an archaic ape-spite, a brosy barbarization!

I am a nationalist only in the sense that the sane Heptarchian
was a Wessexman or a Mercian or what not: temporarily,
opportunistically. I think the Braid Scots may yet give lovely
lights and shadows not only to English but to the perfected
speech of Cosmopolitan Man: so I cultivate it, for lack of
that perfect speech that is yet to be. I think there's the chance
that Scotland, especially in its Glasgow, in its bitter straitening
of the economic struggle, may win to a freedom preparatory
to, and in alignment with, that cosmopolitan freedom, long
before England: so, a cosmopolitan opportunist, I am some
kind of Nationalist. But I'd rather, any day, be an expatriate
writing novels in Persian about the Cape of Good Hope than
a member of a homogeneous literary cultus (to quote again
the cant phrase of the day) prosing eternally on one plane –
the insanitary reactions to death of a Kelvingrove bourgeois,
or the owlish gawk (it would speedily have that seeming) of
Ben Lomond through its clouds, like a walrus through a fuff
of whiskers.

For this Scottish Siva herself, brandishing her many arms
of smoke against the coming of the darkness, it is pleasant to
remember at least one incident. On a raining night six hundred
and fifty years ago a small band of men, selfless and desperate
and coolly-led, tramped through the wynds to the assault of
the English-garrisoned Bell o' the Brae (which is now the
steep upper part of High Street). It was a venture unsupported
by priest or patrician, the intellectual or bourgeois of those
days. It succeeded: and it lighted a flame of liberty throughout
Scotland.

Some day the surgeon-leaders of the hundred and fifty
thousand may take that tale of Bell o' the Brae for their text.

LITERARY LIGHTS

One of the most praiseworthy – praiseworthy in its entertainment value – efforts of the critic has always been his attempt to levitate himself out of himself by the ingenuous method of hauling with great passion upon his own boot-laces. In the words of Mr. Alan Porter 'The critic, before he sets down a word, must beat himself on the head and ask a hundred times, each time more bitterly and searchingly, "And is it true? Is it true?" He must analyse his judgment and make sure that it is nowhere stained or tinted with the blood of his heart. And he must search out a table of values from which he can be certain that he has left nothing unconsidered. If, after all these precautions and torments, he is unable to deliver a true judgment, then fate has been too strong for him; he was never meant to be a critic.'

The present writer was assuredly never meant to be a critic. He has attempted no feats of manipulative surgery upon either his personality or his judgment. He confesses with no shame that the dicta of criticism laid down by Mr. Porter appear to him analogous to the chest-beating posturings of a righteous baboon prior to its robbing an orchard. Flippancy apart, the researches of Bekhterev and Pavlov should have disposed once and for all of such archaic beliefs as the possibility of inhibiting a reflex by incantation. Indeed, it did not require reflexological research (of which the average critic has never heard – or, if he has, imagines it has something to do with the torturing of dogs and Mr. Bernard Shaw) to dispose of this nonsense regarding 'heart' and 'head'. To commit hari-kari may be an admirable and hygienic exercise, but is an operation seldom survived by even the remoter portions of the extra-intestinal anatomy.

Far more serious doubts assail the non-professional critic when he enters upon the study of such a subject as (reputed) Scots letters. If he enters this great library from the open air, not through an underground passage from the book-lined gloom of a study, the piles of stacked volumes are dismaying in their colour and size and plenitude. Only here and there does he recognize a name or a title; the books tower to dim ceilings, are piled in great strata, have the dust of the last few years yet gathered thickly enough upon them. How may he pass judgment? The books he has missed – the books he has never read! What relative importance have the few names and titles in his memory to the hidden values in this great library?

For, in the pressing multitudes of reputedly Scots books which pour from the presses, there may have been a new Melville, a new Typee, a Scots Joyce, a Scots Proust? Nothing impossible in any of those suppositions. The book may have appeared, it failed to be noticed, (as hundreds of good books have failed to be noted,) it was poorly advertised, had inadequate publicity, was overshadowed by the simultaneous publication of a great name – and moulders now its representative copies in two or three libraries while the remainder of the stock – not even 'remaindered' – has returned to the printer for repulping. There is nothing to say that this has not happened very often.

Even if the critic passes a judgment with some fair knowledge of the factors – how of the unpublished books? There may be manuscripts circulating the publishers' offices that sing a new, clear splendid note in letters – sing it so loudly that no publisher's reader can abide the beat of the music in his ears. . . . This is not only possible, but very probable. It was as true of the past as it is of the present, though both gods and machines were of a different order three hundred years ago. Yet even then it is possible that poets dwarfing Shakespeare remained unpublished and unplayed for lack of suitable influences, suitable patronage; and their manuscripts, with the wisdom and delight of the shining minds that begat them, have long mouldered to dust.

The new and unknown Scots writer facing the publishing, printing world has the usual chances and mischances to face in a greater measure than his English compeer. Firstly, in almost every case, he must seek publication in London. Scots publishers are surely amongst the sorriest things that enter hell: their publicity methods are as antique as their format, their houses are generally staffed by those who in Bengali circles would write after their names, and as their chief qualification, 'failed B.A.' (or slightly worse, 'M.A. (St. Andrews)'). He must consign his manuscript to alien publishers and the consideration of largely alien readers.

For, however the average Scots writer believes himself Anglicized, his reaction upon the minds of the intelligent English reader (especially of the professional reader) is curiously similar to that produced by the English poems of Dr. Rabindranath Tagore. The prose – or verse – is impeccably correct, the vocabulary is rich and adequate, the English is severe, serene ... But unfortunately it is not English. The English reader is haunted by a sense of something foreign stumbling and hesitating behind this smooth façade of adequate technique: it is as though the writer did not *write* himself, but *translated* himself.

Often the Scots writer is quite unaware of this essential foreignness in his work; more often, seeking an adequate word or phrase he hears an echo in an alien tongue that would adorn his meaning with a richness, a clarity and a conciseness impossible in orthodox English. That echo is from Braid Scots, from that variation of the Anglo-Saxon speech which was the tongue of the great Scots civilization, the tongue adopted by the basic Pictish strain in Scotland as its chief literary tool.

Further, it is still in most Scots communities, (in one or other Anglicized modification,) the speech of bed and board and street and plough, the speech of emotional ecstasy and emotional stress. But it is not genteel. It is to the bourgeois of Scotland coarse and low and common and loutish, a matter for laughter, well enough for hinds and the like, but for the genteel to be quoted in vocal inverted commas. It is a thing rigorously elided from their serious intercourse – not only with the English, but among themselves. It is seriously believed by such stratum of the Scots populace to be an inadequate and pitiful and blunted implement, so that Mr. Eric Linklater delivers *ex cathedra* judgment upon it as 'inadequate to deal with the finer shades of emotion'.

But for the truly Scots writer it remains a real and a haunting thing, even while he tries his best to forget its existence and to write as a good Englishman. In this lies his tragedy. He has to *learn* to write in English: he is like a Chinese scholar spending the best years of his life in the mystic mazes of the pictographs, and emerging so exhausted from the travail that originality of research or experiment with his new tool is denied him. Consequently, the free and anarchistic experimentations of the progressive members of a free and homogeneous literary cultus are denied him. Nearly every Scots writer of the past writing in orthodox English has been not only incurably second-rate, but incurably behind the times. The Scots discovery of photographic realism in novel-writing, for example – I refer to *Hatter's Castle*, not the very different *House with the Green Shutters* – post-dated the great French and English realists some thirty or forty years. But to the Scot Dr. Cronin's work appeared a very new and terrifying and fascinating thing indeed; to the English public, astounded that anything faintly savouring of accuracy, photographic or otherwise, should come out of Scotland, it was equally amazing. At such rate of progress among the Anglo-Scots one may guess that in another fifty years or so a Scots Virginia Woolf will astound the Scottish scene, a Scots James Joyce electrify it. To expect contemporary experimentation from the Anglo-Scots themselves appears equivalent to expecting a Central African savage in possession of a Birmingham kite to prove capable of inventing a helicopter.

Consciousness of this inferiority of cultural position within the English tradition is a very definite thing among the younger generation of Anglo-Scots writers of to-day. Their most characteristic organ, *The Modern Scot,* is a constant reiteration of protest. Owned and edited by one of those genial Englishmen in search of a revolution who have added to the gaiety of nations from Ireland to Uganda, *The Modern Scot* has set itself, strictly within the English tradition, to out-English the English. As one who on a lonely road doth walk with fear and dread, very conscious of the frightful fiend who close behind doth tread, it marches always a full yard ahead of extremist English opinion – casting the while an anxious backward glance. It decries the children of 'naturalism' with a praiseworthy but unnatural passion, championing in their place, with a commendable care for pathology, the idiot offspring begat on the modern literary scene in such numbers from the incestuous unions of Strindberg and Dr. Freud. It is eclectic to quite an obscure degree, is incapable of an article that does not quote either Proust or Paul Einzig, and raises an approving voice in praise of the joyous, if infantile tauromachic obsessions of Mr. Roy Campbell. Its motif-note, indeed, is literary Fascism – to the unimpassioned, if astounded, eye it would seem as if all the Fascist undergraduates of Scotland these days were hastening, in pimples and a passion for sophistication, to relieve themselves of a diarrhoetic Johnsonese in the appropriate privy of *The Modern Scot.* The entire being of the periodical, however, is rather an exhibitory, or sanitary, exercise, than a contributing factor towards authentic experimentation.

With a few exceptions presently to be noted, there is not the remotest reason why the majority of modern Scots writers should be considered Scots at all. The protagonists of the Scots literary Renaissance deny this. They hold, for example, that Norman Douglas or Compton Mackenzie, though they write in English and deal with un-Scottish themes, have nevertheless an essential Scottishness which differentiates them from the native English writer. In exactly the same manner, so had

Joseph Conrad an essential Polishness. But few (except for the purpose of exchanging diplomatic courtesies) pretend that Conrad was a Polish writer, to be judged as a Pole. He wrote brilliantly and strangely and beautifully in English; so does Mr. Norman Douglas, so does Mr. Cunninghame Graham. Mention of the latter is peculiarly to the point. Mr. Graham has, I believe, a large modicum of Spanish blood in his veins, he writes much of Spanish or Spanish-American subjects, and his word-manipulation is most certainly not of the English orthodox. But we have still to hear of Spain acclaiming him one of her great essayists.

The admirable plays of Dr. James Bridie – such as *Tobias and the Angel* or the unforgettable *Jonah and the Whale* – have been hailed in Scotland as examples of modern Scots drama. They are excellent examples – but not of Scots drama. They are examples of how an Englishman, hailing from Scotshire, can write excellent plays. Mr. Edwin Muir writes poems of great loveliness; so does Mr. Roy Campbell; both are of Scots origin: ergo, great Scots poetry. Dumas père had negro blood in his veins and wrote excellent romances in French: ergo, great negro romance.

That such a position is untenable is obvious. Modern Scotland, the Gaels included, is a nation almost entirely lacking a Scottish literary output. There are innumerable versifiers, ranging from Dr. Charles Murray downwards to Mr. W. H. Hamilton (he of the eldritch glamour); there are hardly more than two poets; and there is no novelist at all. To be oneself a provincial or an alien and to write a book in which the characters infect one's literary medium with a tincture of dialect is not to assist in the creation or continuation of a separate national literature – else Eden Philpotts proves the great, un-English soul of Dartmoor and Tennyson in *The Northern Farmer* was advocating Home Rule for Yorkshire. The chief Literary Lights which modern Scotland claims to light up the scene of her night are in reality no more than the commendable writers of the interesting English county of Scotshire.

Let us consider Mrs. Naomi Mitchison. She is the one writer of the 'historical' novel in modern English who commands respect and enthusiasm. Her pages are aglow with a fine essence of apprehended light. *The Conquered* and *Black Sparta* light up the human spirit very vividly and truly. And they are in no sense Scots books though written by a Scotswoman. Their author once wrote that had she had the command of Scots speech possessed by Lewis Grassic Gibbon she would have written her Spartan books (at least) in Scots. Had she done so they would undoubtedly have been worse novels – but they *would* have been Scots books by a Scots writer, just as the worst of Finnish peasant studies *are* Finnish peasant studies, infinitesimal by the side of Dostoieffski or Tolstoi, but un-Russian in language and content.

Another writer hailed as a great Scots novelist is Mr. Neil Gunn. The acclamation is mistaken. Mr. Gunn is a brilliant novelist from Scotshire who chooses his home county as the scene of his tales. His technique is almost unique among the writers of Scotshire in its effortless efficiency: he moulds beauty in unforgettable phrases – there are things in *The Lost Glen* and *Sun Circle* comparable to the best in the imaginative literature of any school or country. He has probably scarcely yet set out on his scaling of the heights. . . . But they are not the heights of Scots literature; they are not even the pedestrian levels. More in Gunn than in any other contemporary Anglo-Scot (with the exception, perhaps, of George Blake, in a very different category from Gunn, and the finest of the Anglo-Scots realists) the reader seems to sense the haunting foreignness in an orthodox English; he is the greatest loss to itself Scottish literature has suffered in this century. Had his language been Gaelic or Scots there is no doubt of the space or place he would have occupied in even such short study as this. Writing in orthodox English, he is merely a brilliantly unorthodox Englishman.

Once again, a writer who has been hailed as distinctively Scots, Mrs. Willa Muir. So far she has written only two

novels – *Imagined Corners* and *Mrs. Ritchie* – and both show a
depth and distinction, a sheer and splendidly un-womanly
power which stir even the most jaded of enthusiasms. They
suffer, perhaps, from the author's learnings and erudition-
gatherings in the dull hag-forests of the German psychoanalysts,
just as Neil Gunn's *Sun Circle* suffers from a crude and out-dated
concept of history and the historical processes. But that
psychoanalyst obsession is the common leprosy over all
contemporary European imaginative literature, and Mrs.
Muir's strength of spirit and true integrity of vision may yet
transcend it. She has promise of becoming a great artist. But
a great English artist. The fact that she is Scots herself and
deals with Scots scenes and Scots characters is (to drive home
the point ad nauseam) entirely irrelevant from the point of
view of Scots literature: if she were a modern Mexican writing
in Spanish and her scene was Mexico and her peasants spoke
bastardized Nahuatl, would we call it a triumph of Aztec
letters?

Mr. John Buchan has been called the Dean of Scots letters.
Mr. Buchan writes mildly exhilarating romances in the vein
of the late Rider Haggard (though without either Haggard's
magnificent poetic flair or his imaginative grasp), commendable essays on a variety of topics, uninspired if competent
biographies of Sir Walter Scott, the Marquis of Montrose,
and the like distinguished cadaverlitter on the ancient Scottish
scene. He writes it all in a competent, skilful and depressing
English: when his characters talk Scots they do it in suitable
inverted commas: and such characters as do talk Scots are
always the simple, the proletarian, the slightly ludicrous
characters.

Mr. Buchan represents no more than the great, sound,
bourgeois heart of Scotshire. He has written nothing which
has the least connection with Scots literature except a few
pieces of verse – if verse *has* any connection with literature.
In compiling *The Northern Muse,* however, a representative
anthology of Scots 'Vernacular' poetry, he turned aside from

other pursuits to render a real service to what might have been his native literary language. Yet even in that service he could envisage Braid Scots as being only a 'vernacular', the tongue of *a home-reared slave.*

Mrs. Catherine Carswell is among the most interesting of the Anglo-Scots. Her *Life of Robert Burns* was one of the most unique and innocently mendacious studies of the subject ever attempted; her *Savage Pilgrimage* (which met such a sad fate in the teeth of the enraged Mr. Middleton Murry) contributed as little to our knowledge of D. H. Lawrence as it contributed greatly to our knowledge of its author. With such a personality and philosophy much more may be heard of Catherine Carswell: that the philosophy of her school appears a strange and repulsve one, as strange an aberration of the human spirit as history has ever known, merely adds a pathological to a genuine literary interest in her development. Scots letters represses its death-rattle to wave her on with a regretful relief.

Prior to writing *Hatter's Castle, Three Loves,* and *Grand Canary* Dr. A. J. Cronin descended five hundred collieries on tours of inspection. As a consequence he is notable for a kind of inky immensity, and an interestingly Latinized barbarization of the English language. While *Hatter's Castle* had a Scots scene its characters were gnomes from the sooty deeps of the less salubrious regions of myth: though acclaimed as great and realistic portraits. In *Three Loves* Dr. Cronin showed a disposition to prove uneasy on the Scottish scene; in *Grand Canary* he escaped it entirely, taking his place (probably a permanent place) among the English writers of an order comparable to Miss Mannin or Mr. Gilbert Frankau. He is also the author of a history of aneurism.

Sir James George Frazer, a Scotsman by birth, is the author of the immense *Golden Bough,* a collection of anthropological studies. The author's methods of correlation have been as crude and unregulated as his industry and the cultivation of his erudition have been immense. The confusion of savage and primitive states of culture commenced by Tylor and his school has been carried to excess in the works of Sir J. G. Frazer. From the point of view of the social historian attempting to disentangle the story of man's coming and growth upon this planet he is one of the most calamitous phenomena in modern research: he has smashed in the ruin of pre-history with a coal-hammer, collected every brick disclosed when the dust settled on the débris, and then labelled the exhibits with the assiduous industry of a literary ant. His pleasing literary style in that labelling is in orthodox English.

Mr. Eric Linklater is a lost Norseman with a disposition to go Berserk amidst the unfamiliar trappings of literary civiliza-tion. This disposition came to a head in *The Men of Ness*, a story of the vikings and their raids into the regions of stern guffawdom and unpronunciability. It is a pity that this dis-position should be let loose by the author of *Juan in America*, – in the genre of Mark Twain's *Tramp Abroad*, and one of the most acute and amusing picaresque studies ever perpetrated by the literary farceur. It would be even more regrettable if Mr. Linklater hampered his genius by an uneasy adherence to a so-called Scots literary Renaissance.[1]

Miss Muriel Stuart is one of the very few great poets writing in non-experimental English. She has a comprehension and a lyric beauty almost unknown to this English day: the deep passion of her poems in *Christ at Carnival* shines the more finely in that they lack the ornate imagery of Francis Thompson. One of the most magic lines in a memory prolific in the waste amusement of collecting magic lines (as is the present writer's) is her '*A thin hail ravened against the doors of dark.*' Miss Stuart, of Scots origin, has been hailed as a great Scots poet. She is as little Scots as Dante.

Yet Miss Stuart's genius brings us at last to consideration of the two solitary lights in modern Scots Literature. They rise from men who are writers in both Scots and in English –

---

[1] This fear has been pleasingly dispelled with the publication of the excellent *Magnus Merriman*.

very prolific and controversial writers, men occupied with politics and economic questions, poets in the sense that life, not editors or anthologists, demand of them their poetry. But for the fact that this paper has been devoted largely to an argument that should have needed no enforcing, the work of these two would have occupied almost all the space under such heading as Literary Lights. One of these two is Hugh MacDiarmid and the other Lewis Spence.

MacDiarmid's poetry in Braid Scots came upon a world which had grown accustomed to the belief that written Scots was a vehicle for the more flat-footed sentiments of the bothy only; it came upon a world pale and jaded with the breathing and rebreathing in the same room of the same stagnant air of orthodox English. He demonstrated, richly and completely, and continues to demonstrate, the flexibility and the loveliness of that alien variation of the Anglo-Saxon speech which is Braid Scots. The first of MacDiarmid that the present writer encountered was something which still lingers in his mind (unreasonably, considering the magnificent *To Circumjack Cencrastus* or the sweeping majesty of the *Hymns to Lenin*):

'Ae weet forenicht i' the yow-trummle
   I saw you antrin thing,
A watergaw wi' its chitterin' licht
   Ayont the on-ding;
An' I thocht o' the last wild look ye gied
   Afore ye dee'd!

There was nae reek i' the laverock's hoose
   That nicht – an' nane i' mine;
But I hae thocht o' that foolish licht
   Ever sin' syne;
An' I think that maybe at last I ken
   What your look meant then.'

This is probably, in Mr. MacDiarmid's own view, no more than light versification. But it is certainly not English versification; the prisoner behind the polished walls has escaped

and engaged himself in the moulding of a curious façade. Mr.
MacDiarmid, like all great poets, has his in and out moments –
some of them disastrous moments; his care to set this planet
aright has laid waste some of his finest poems – but, working
in that medium of Braid Scots which he calls synthetic Scots,
he has brought Scots language into print again as a herald
in tabard, not the cap-and-bells clown of romantic versification.

Of an entirely different order, but a genius no less genuine,
is Mr. Spence in his Scots poetry. To show the width and
sweep of Braid Scots from MacDiarmid to Spence, it is
necessary to quote only:

'Time that has dinged doun castels and hie toures,
And cast great crouns like tinsel in the fire,
That halds his hand for palace nor for byre,
Stands sweir at this, the oe of Venus' boures,

Not Time himself can dwell withouten floures,
Though aiks maun fa' the rose shall bide entire;
So sall this diamant of a queen's desire
Outflourish all the stanes that Time devours.'

How far these two are isolated phenomena, how far the
precursors of a definite school of Scots literature is still un-
certain: they have their imitators in full measure: in William
Soutar the Elijah of MacDiarmid may yet have an Elisha.
When, if ever, the majority of Scots poets – not versifiers –
begin to use Braid Scots as a medium that dream of a Scots
literary renaissance may tread the *via terrena* of fulfilment,
enriching (in company with orthodox English) the literary
heritage of that language of Cosmopolis towards which the
whole creation moves.

An experiment of quite a different order from MacDiarmid's
writing in synthetic Scots, or Spence's in deliberate excavation
in the richness of the antique Scots vocabularies, may be noted
here. As already stated, there is no novelist, (or, indeed prose
writer,) worthy of the name who is writing in Braid Scots.
The technique of Lewis Grassic Gibbon in his trilogy *A Scots*

Quair – of which only Parts I and II, *Sunset Song* and *Cloud Howe*, have yet been published – is to mould the English language into the rhythms and cadences of Scots spoken speech, and to inject into the English vocabulary such minimum number of words from Braid Scots as that remodelling requires. His scene so far has been a comparatively uncrowded and simple one – the countryside and village of modern Scotland. Whether his technique is adequate to compass and express the life of an industrialized Scots town in all its complexity is yet to be demonstrated; whether his peculiar style may not become either intolerably mannered or degenerate, in the fashion of Joyce, into the unfortunate unintelligibilities of a literary second childhood, is also in question.

For the Gaels, one cannot do better than quote James Barke, the author of *The World his Pillow* and *The Wild MacRaes*, and himself a remarkable Anglo-Gael:

'In Scotland to-day there exists no body of Gaelic culture. In the realms of imaginative literature – in fiction and drama – there is little or no original work in evidence; and what does exist is of poor quality and vitiated by a spineless sentimentality.

'In verse alone the modern Gaelic writer would seem to find a suitable medium for expression – Donald Sinclair (died recently); Duncan Johnston of Islay; John MacFadyen. MacFadyen, I believe, has it. But here too the output is small and fragmentary and, in quality, perhaps best compared to the Poet's Corner of the provincial press.

'There is no one to-day in any way approaching the stature of the great Gaelic poets: Alasdair MacMhaighistir Alasdair and Duncan Ban MacIntyre – or even Alexander MacDonald or Ewan MacColl.

'The reason for the poverty of contemporary Gaelic culture is not difficult to state.

'When the Young Pretender and his Highland forces were defeated on Culloden Moor in 1746, there followed a ruthless military occupation of the Highland. The clan system was broken up and all forms of Gaelic culture were suppressed. The ownership of partly communal land passed into the hands of a small group of private individuals. The land was soon cleared of its human population. With the exception of a few impoverished crofting communities the native Gael became subservient to the dominant land-owning class.

'First military suppression and dictatorship, then economic suppression were the cause of the decay of the Gael and his native Gaelic culture. From the field of Culloden to the first National Government economic, and consequently racial, decay has continued steadily. In the modern capitalist state the Gael finds himself an anachronism – almost an extinct species. The few of them who are articulate turn, therefore, to a hopeless backward looking, backward longing. A decayed race, lingering over-long on a decayed economic system, can produce only a decayed culture.

'The present attempts to revive this culture are necessarily doomed to failure. In its hey-day, Gaelic culture was surprisingly beautiful and vital. As part of Scotland's cultural heritage it will survive for its richness and beauty. But a people can no more live on the glories of the past than it can survive on the memories of its last meal.

'The death rattle of Gaelic culture may be amplified by all sorts of bodies and committees. They delude themselves, however, in thinking that by so doing they are performing an act of resurrection. . . .

'Fionn MacColla, in English, it may be noted, is far away the finest example of the Gaelic influence. In a very profound sense, his English is the finest Gaelic we have.'

Sic itur ad astra.

THE LAND

I. WINTER

I like the story of the helpful Englishman who, when shown a modern Scots Nationalist map with 'Scotland Proper' stretching from John o' Groats to the Tweed, and 'Scotia Irredenta' stretching from the Tweed to the Mersey, suggested 'Scotland Improper' in place of the latter term. The propriety of Northern England to rank as a section of Scotland may have political justice; it certainly has no æsthetic claim. If I look out on the land of Scotland and see it fouled by the smoking slag-heaps of industrialism rightwards and leftwards, a long trailing rift down the eastern coast and a vomiting geyser in Lanarkshire, I feel no stirrings of passion at all to add those tortured wastes of countryside, Northumbria and Lancashire, to the Scottish land. I like the grey glister of sleet in the dark this night, seen through the unblinded window; and I like this idle task of voyaging with a pen through the storm-happed wastes of Scotland in winter; but I balk at reaching beyond the Border, into that chill land of alien geology and deplorable methods of ploughing. This paraffin lamp set beside me on the table was lit for the benefit of myself and Scotland Proper: I shrink from geographical impropriety to-night as my Kailyard literary forerunners shrank from description of the bridal bed.

And now that I bend to the task and the logs are crackling so cheerfully and the wind has veered a point, and there's a fine whoom in the lum, it comes on me with a qualm that perhaps I have no qualifications for the task at all. For if the land is the enumeration of figures and statistics of the yield of wheat in the Merse or the Carse of Gowrie, fruit-harvesting in Coupar-Angus, or how they couple and breed their cattle in Ayrshire, I am quite lost. And if the land is the lilting of tourist names, Strathmore, Ben Lomond, Ben Macdhui, Rannoch, Loch Tay and the Sidlaw Hills, I confess to bored glimpses of this and that stretch of unique countryside, I confess that once (just such a night as this) I journeyed up to Oban; and the train was bogged in a snowstorm; and I spent shivering hours in view of Ben Cruachan; and once an Anglo-Gaelic novelist took me round Loch Lomond in his car and we drank good whisky and talked about Lenin; and an uncle once dragged me, protesting, up Lochnagar, in search of a sunrise that failed to appear – the sun hid that morning in a diffusion of peasoup fog; and I've viewed the Caledonian Canal with suitable commercial enthusiasm and recited (as a small boy at concerts) verse about the Dee and Don, they still run on (a phenomenon which elicited complacent clappings of commendation from my audiences); and I've eaten trout by Loch Levenside. But I refuse the beetling crags and the spume of Spey; still I think they are not The Land.

That is The Land out there, under the sleet, churned and pelted there in the dark, the long rigs upturning their clayey faces to the spear-onset of the sleet. That is The Land, a dim vision this night of laggard fences and long stretching rigs. And the voice of it – the true and unforgettable voice – you can hear even such a night as this as the dark comes down, the immemorial plaint of the peewit, flying lost. *That* is The Land – though not quite all. Those folk in the byre whose lantern light is a glimmer through the sleet as they muck and bed and tend the kye, and milk the milk into tin pails, in curling froth – they are The Land in as great a measure. Those two, a dual power, are the protagonists in this little sketch. They are the essentials for the title. And besides, quite unfairly, they are all so intimately mine that I would give them that position though they had not a shadow of a claim to it.

I like to remember I am of peasant rearing and peasant stock. Good manners prevail on me not to insist on the fact over-much, not to boast in the company of those who come from manses and slums and castles and villas, the folk of the proletariat, the bigger and lesser bourgeoisies. But I am again and again, as I hear them talk of their origins and beginnings and begetters, conscious of an overweening pride that mine was thus and so, that the land was so closely and intimately mine (my mother used to hap me in a plaid in harvest-time and leave me in the lee of a stook while she harvested) that I feel of a strange and antique age in the company and converse of my adult peers – like an adult himself listening to the bright sayings and laughters of callow boys, parvenus on the human scene, while I, a good Venriconian Pict, harken from the shade of my sun circle and look away, bored, in pride of possession at my terraced crops, at the on-ding of rain and snow across my leavened fields . . . .

How much this is merely reaction from the hatreds of my youth I do not know. For once I had a very bitter detestation for all this life of the land and the folk upon it. My view was that of my distant cousin, Mr. Leslie Mitchell, writing in his novel *The Thirteenth Disciple*:

'A grey, grey life. Dull and grey in its routine, Spring, Summer, Autumn, Winter, that life the Neolithic men brought from the south, supplanting Azilian hunger and hunting and light-hearted shiftlessness with servitude to seasons and soil and the tending of cattle. A beastly life. With memory of it and reading those Catholic writers, who, for some obscure reason, champion the peasant and his state as the ideal state, I am moved to unkindly mirth . . . unprintably sceptical as to Mr. Chesterton or his chelas ever having grubbed a livelihood from hungry acres of red clay, or regarding the land and its inhabitants with other vision than an obese Victorian astigmatism.'

Not, I think, that I have gone the full circle and have returned among the romantics. As I listen to that sleet-drive I can see the wilting hay-ricks under the fall of the sleet and think of the wind ablow on ungarmented floors, ploughmen in sodden bothies on the farms outbye, old, bent and wrinkled people who have mislaid so much of fun and hope and high endeavour in grey servitude to those rigs curling away, only half-inanimate, into the night. I can still think and see these things with great clarity though I sit in this warm room and write this pleasant essay and find pleasure in the manipulation of words on a blank page. But when I read or hear our new leaders and their plans for making of Scotland a great peasant nation, a land of little farms and little farming communities, I am moved to a bored disgust with those pseudo-literary romantics playing with politics, those refugees from the warm parlours and lights and policemen and theatre-stalls of the Scots cities. They are promising the New Scotland a purgatory that would decimate it. They are promising it narrowness and bitterness and heart-breaking toil in one of the most unkindly agricultural lands in the world. They are promising to make of a young, ricketic man, with the phthisis of Glasgow in his throat, a bewildered labourer in pelting rains and the flares of head-aching suns, they are promising him years of a murderous monotony, poverty and struggle and loss of happy human relationships. They promise that of which they know nothing, except through sipping of the scum of Kailyard romance.

For this life is for no modern man or woman – even the finest of these. It belongs to a different, an alien generation. That winter that is sweeping up the Howe, bending the whins on Auchindreich hill, seeping with pelting blasts through the old walls of Edzell Castle, malagarousing the ploughed lands and swashing about and above the heavy cattle-courts where in darkness the great herds lie cudchewing and breath-blowing in frosty steam, is a thing for most to be stared at, tourist-wise, endured for a day or a week. This night, the winter on the countryside, the crofter may doze contentedly in the arm-chair in the ingleneuk and the mistress yawn with an equal content at the clock. For you or I or young Simon who is taking his girl to the pictures it is as alien and unendurable in permanence as the life of the Kamtchatkan.

Going down the rigs this morning, my head full of that un-
accustomed smell of the earth, fresh and salty and anciently
mouldy, I remembered the psalmist's voice of the turtle and
instinctively listened for its Scots equivalent – that far cooing
of pigeons that used to greet the coming of Spring mornings
when I was a boy. But the woods have gone, their green
encirclement replaced by swathes of bog and muck and rank-
growing heath, all the land about here is left bare in the
North wind's blow. The pigeons have gone and the rabbits
and like vermin multiplied – unhappily and to no profit, for
the farmers tell me the rabbits are tuberculous, dangerous
meat. Unshielded by the woods, the farm-lands are assailed
by enemies my youth never knew.

But they are fewer and fewer, the cultivated lands. Half of
them are in grass – permanently in grass – and browsed upon
by great flocks of sheep, leaving that spidertrail of grey that
sheep bring to pastures. We are repeating here what the Border
men did in Badenoch and the Highlands – eating away the
land and the crofter, killing off the peasant as surely as in
Russia – and with no Russian compensation. If the little
dykes and the sodden ditches that rivuleted in the Springs of
bygone times with the waters hastening to the Forthie – the
ditches that separated this little farm from that – were filled
and obliterated by a sovkholz with tractors and high enthusiasm and a great and tremendous agricultural hope, I at least
could turn to the hills and the heath – that other and older
Land – with no more regret than the sensitive felt in the
passing of the windjammers and the coming of the steamboats.
But instead there has come here only a brainless greed, a
grabbing stupidity, the mean avariciousness and planlessness
of our community in epitome. I do not wonder that the rabbits
are tuberculous: the wonder is that they are not jaundiced as
well.

It was then that I thought what a fine and heartsome smell

has rank cow-dung as the childe with the graip hurls it steady heap on heap from the rear of his gurling cart. They sell stuff in Paris in little bottles with just that smell, and charge for it handsomely, as they may well do, for it is the smell that back-grounds existence. And then (having come to the end of the rig and looked at the rabbit-snare and found it empty and found also a stone whereon to sit) I fell into another meditation: this dung that backgrounded existence, this Autumn's crops, meal for the folk of the cities, good heartsome barley alcohol – would never be spread, never be seeded, never gound to bree, but for the aristocracy of the earth, the ploughmen and the peasants. These are the real rulers of Scotland: they are the rulers of the earth!

And how patient and genial and ingenuously foulmouthed and dourly wary and kindly they are, those selfless aristos of Scotland. They endure a life of mean and bitter poverty, an order sneered upon by the little folk of the towns, their gait is a mockery in city streets, you see little waitresses stare haughtily at their great red, suncreased hands, plump professors in spectacles and pimples enunciate theses on their mortality and morality, their habits of breeding and their shiftlessness – and they endure it all! They endure the chatter of the city salons, the plannings of this and that war and blockade, they endure the pretensions of every social class but their own to be the mainspring and base of human society – they, the masters, who feed the world! . . . And it came on me that all over Great Britain, all over Europe this morning, the mean fields of France and fat pastures of Saxony and the rolling lands of Roumania those rulers of the earth were out and about, bent-backed at plodding toil, the world's great Green International awaiting the coming of its Spartacus.

There are gulls in from the sea this morning, wheeling in comet tails at the heels of this and that ploughman, a dotting of signatures against the dark green of the Bervie braes. Here the land is red clay, sour and dour, but south, by Brechin, you come to that rich loam land that patterns Scotland like a ragged veil, the lovely land that even here erupts in sudden patches and brings tall corn while the surrounding fields wilt in the baking clay. The clay is good for potatoes in the dry years, however – those dry years that come every decade or so for no reason that we know of here in the Howe, for we are beyond the 'mountain-shadow' that makes of Donside and Braemar the tourist's camping-ground. . . .

In the sunlight, down by Kinneff, the fog-horn has begun its wail, the sun has drawn great banks of mist out of the North Sea and now they are billowing over Auchendreich like the soft, coloured spume from a washing-tub. But leftwards the sun is a bright, steely glare on the ridged humps of the Grampians, hastening south into the coming of Summer, crowned with snow in their upper haughs – much the same mountains, I suppose, as the Maglemosians looked on that Spring day in the youth of the world and the youth of Scotland when they crossed the low lands of the Dogger Bank and clambered up the rocks of Kinneff into a still and untenanted Scotland. The great bear watched them come, and the eagle from his Grampian eyrie and scattering packs of wolves on the forest fringes saw that migration of the hunters seven thousand years ago. They came over Auchendreich there, through the whins and heath, and halted and stared at the billowing Howe, and laughed and muttered and squatted and stared – dark men, and tall, without gods or kings, classes or culture, writers or artists, free and happy, and all the world theirs. Scotland woke and looked at them from a hundred peaks and stared a shy virgin's amaze.

All winter the cattle were kept to the byres. This morning saw their first deliverance – cows and stirks and stots and calves they grumphed and galumphed from the byre to the park and squattered an astounded delight in the mud, and boxed at each other, and stared a bovine surprise at the world, and went mad with delight and raced round the park, and stood still and mooed: they mooed on a long, devilish note, the whole lot of them, for nearly two minutes on end and for no reason at all but delight in hearing their own moo. They are all of mixed breed, except one, a small Jersey cow of a southron coldness, who drops her aitches, haughtily, and also her calves. The strains are mostly shorthorn, with a dash of Highland, I suspect: a hundred years of mixed pasturing and crop-rotation weeded out the experimental breeds and left these satisfying mongrels. Presently (after racing a grocer's cart for the length of the field and all but hamstringing themselves on the boundary fence) they abandoned playfulness and took to grazing, remembering their mission was to provide fat carcases for the slaughter-shed——

We balk from such notions, in Spring especially, in especial as the evening comes with that fresh smell all about it, impregnating it, the kind of evening that has growth and youngness and kindliness in its essence – balk from the thought of our strange, unthinking cruelties, the underpit of blood and suffering and intolerable horror on which the most innocent of us build our lives. I feel this evening that never again will I eat a dead animal (or, I find myself guarding the resolve with the inevitable flippancy, a live one). But that resolve will be gone to-morrow: the Horror is beyond personalism, very old and strange and terrible. Even those hunters all those millenia ago were eaters of flesh.

It is strange to think that, if events never die (as some of the wise have supposed,) but live existence all time in Eternity, back through the time-spirals, still alive and aware in that world seven thousand years ago, the hunters are *now* lying down their first night in Scotland, with their tall, deep-bosomed sinewy mates and their children, tired from trek. . . . Over in the west a long line of lights twinkles against the dark. Whin-burning – or the camps of Maglemose?

III. SUMMER

I cycled up the Glen of Drumtochty to-day. It was very hot, the heat was caught in the cup of the Howe and spun and stirred there, milkily, by little currents of wind that had come filtering down through the Grampian passes. In the long, dusty stretches of roadway my shadow winked and fluttered perspiringly while I followed in a sympathetic sweat. This till we passed down into Glen itself, when the overshadowing hills flung us a cool shade. There the water sparkled and spun coolly, so coldly, a little burn with deep brown detritus winding amidst the broom and the whins. To the left the reafforested Drumtochty Hill towered up dazzlingly impossible in purple. This Tyrian splendour on Drumtochty Hill is probably un-matched in all Scotland, very breath-taking and strange, alien to Scotland: it is a wonder, a flamboyant flaunting of nature that comes for a month on our dour hill-lands and we stare at it, sober, Presbyterian, from our blacks and browns – much as MacDiarmid visioned the Scots on Judgment Day staring at

'God and a' his gang
O' angels in the lift,
Thae trashy, bleezin' French-like folk
Wha garred them shift. . . .'

Beyond the contours of Drumtochty, through the piping of that stillness, snipe were sounding. I got off my bicycle to listen to that and look round. So doing I was aware of a sober fact: that indeed all this was a little disappointing. I would never apprehend its full darkly colourful beauty until I had gone back to England, far from it, down in the smooth pastures of Hertfordshire some night I would remember it and itch to write of it, I would see it without the unessentials – sweat and flies and that hideous gimcrack castle, nestling – (Good God, it even *nestled!*) among the trees. I would see it in simplicity then, even as I would see the people of the land.

This perhaps is the real land; not those furrows that haunt me as animate. This is the land, unstirred and greatly untouched by men, unknowing ploughing or crops or the coming of the scythe. Yet even those hills were not always thus. The Archaic Civilization came here and terraced great sections of those

hills and reared Devil Stones, Sun Circles, to the great agricultural gods of ancient times – long ago, before Pytheas sailed
these coasts, while Alexander rode his horse across the Jaxartes
there were peasants on those hills, on such a day as this, who
paused to wipe the sweat from their faces and look with
shrewd eyes at the green upspringing of the barley crops. . . .
By night they slept in houses dug in the earth, roofed with
thatch, and looked out on a wilder and wetter Howe, but
still with that passion of purple mantling it in this month.
They are so tenuous and yet so real, those folk – and how
they haunted me years ago! I had no great interest in the
things around me, I remember, the summer dawns that came
flecked with saffron over the ricks of my father's farm, the
whisper and pelt of the corn-heads, green turning to yellow
in the long fields that lay down in front of our front-door,
the rattle and creak of the shelvins of a passing box-cart, the
chirp and sardonic *Ay!* of the farming childe who squatted
unshaven, with twinkling eyes, on the forefront of the shelvin
. . . but the ancient men haunted those woods and hills for me,
and do so still.

I climbed up the top of Cairn o' Mount with my bicycle
and sat and lunched and looked about me: and found it very
still, the land of Scotland taking a brief siesta in that midday
hour. Down in the north the green parks, miles away, were
like plaques of malachite set on the table of some craftsman of
ancient Chichen-Itza or Mexico, translucent and gleaming
and polished. One understood then, if never before, how that
colour – green – obsessed the ancient civilization with its
magic virtues. It was one of the colours that marked a Giver
of Life – reasonably, for those crops are surely such Givers?
It is better land here than in my homeland – darker, streaked
with clay, but with a richer sub-soil. Between the green of the
corn and barley shone the darker stretches of the tattie-shaws,
the turnip tops, and the honey brown of the clover. Bees were
humming about me: one came and ate jam from my sand-
wiches, some discontented apian soul unfulfilled with the

natural honey of the heather-bells and longing for the tart, sharp tastes of the artificial.

He is not alone in that. In the days of my youth (I have that odd pleasure that men in the early thirties derive from thinking of themselves as beyond youth: this pleasure fades in the forties) men and women still lived largely on the food-stuffs grown in the districts – kale and cabbage and good oatmeal, they made brose and porridge and crisp oatcakes, and jams from the blackberry bushes in the dour little, sour little gardens. But that is mostly a matter of the past. There are few who bake oatcakes nowadays, fewer still who ever taste kale. Stuff from the grocer's, stuff in bottles and tins, the canned nutriments of Chicago and the ubiquitous Fray Bentos, have supplanted the old-time diets. This dull, feculent stuff is more easy to deal with, not enslaving your whole life as once the cooking and serving did in the little farms and cottars' houses – cooking in the heat of such a day as this on great open fireplaces, without even a range. And though I sit here on this hill and deplore the fusionless foods of the canneries, I have no sympathy at all with those odd souls of the cities who would see the return of that 'rich agricultural life' as the return of something praiseworthy, blessed and rich and generous. Better Fray Bentos and a seat in the pictures with your man of a Saturday night than a grilling baking of piled oatcakes and a headache withal.

They change reluctantly, the men and women of the little crofts and cottar houses; but slowly a quite new orientation of outlook is taking place. There are fewer children now plodding through the black glaur of the wet summer storms to school, fewer in both farm and cottar house. The ancient, strange whirlimagig of the generations that enslaved the Scots peasantry for centuries is broken. In times gone by a ploughman might save and scrape and live meanly and hardly and marry a quean of like mettle. And in time they would have gathered enough to rent a croft, then a little farm; and all the while they saved, and lived austere, sardonic lives; and their savings took them at last to the wide cattle-courts and the great stone-floored kitchen of a large farm. And all the while the woman bred, very efficiently and plentifully and without fuss – twelve or thirteen were the common numberings of a farmer's progeny. And those children grew up, and their father died. And in the division of property at his death each son or daughter gathered as inheritance only a few poor pounds. And perforce they started as ploughmen in the bothies, maids in the kitchens, and set about climbing the rungs again – that their children might do the same.

It kept a kind of democracy on the land that is gone or is going; your halflin or your maid was the son or the daughter of your old friends of High Rigs: your own sons and daughters were in bothies or little crofts: it was a perfect Spenglerian cycle. Yet it was waste effort, it was as foolish as the plod of an ass in a treadmill, innumerable generations of asses. If the clumsy fumblements of contraception have done no more than break the wheel and play of that ancient cycle they have done much. Under these hills – so summer-hazed, so immobile and essentially unchanging – of a hundred years hence I do not know what strange master of the cultivated lands will pass in what strange mechanical contrivance: but he will be outwith that ancient yoke, and I send him my love and the hope that he'll sometime climb up Cairn o' Mount and sit where I'm sitting now, and stray in summery thought – into the sun-hazed mists of the future, into the lives and wistful desirings of forgotten men who begat him.

IV. AUTUMN

I have a daughter four years old who was born in England and goes to school there, and already has notions on ethnology. Occasionally she and I debate and fall out, and her final triumphant thrust is 'You're only Scotch!'

Autumn of all seasons is when I realize how very Scotch I am, how interwoven with the fibre of my body and personality is this land and its queer, scarce harvests, its hours of reeking sunshine and stifling rain, how much a stranger I am, south, in those seasons of mist and mellow fruitfulness as alien to my Howe as the olive groves of Persia. It is a harder and slower harvest, and lovelier in its austerity, that is gathered here, in September's early coming, in doubtful glances on the sky at dawn, in listening to the sigh of the sea down there by Bervie. Mellow it certainly is not: but it has the most unique of tangs, this season haunted by the laplaplap of the peesie's wings, by great moons that come nowhere as in Scotland, unending moons when the harvesting carts plod through great thickets of fir-shadow to the cornyards deep in glaur.

These are the most magical nights of the land: they endure but a little while, but their smells – sharp and clear, commingled of fresh horse-dung and dusty cornheads – pervade the winter months. The champ and showd of a horse in that moonsprayed dark and the guttural 'Tchkh, min!' of the forker, the great shapes of cattle in the parks as you ride by, the glimmer far away of the lights of some couthy toun on the verge of sleep, the queer shapes of post and gate and stook – Nature unfolds the puppets and theatre pieces year after year, unvaryingly, and they lose their dust, each year uniquely fresh. You can stand and listen as though for the lost trumpet of God in that autumn night silence: but indeed all that you are listening for is a passing peewit.

It is strange how Scotland has no Gilbert White or H. J. Massingham to sing its fields, its birds, such night as this, to chronicle the comings and goings of the swallows in simple, careful prose, ecstasy controlled. But perhaps not so strange. We Scots have little interest in the wild and its world; I realize how compassed and controlled is my own interest, I am vague about sparrows and tits, martins and swallows, I know little of their seasons, and my ignorance lies heavily upon me not at all. I am concerned so much more deeply with men and women, with their nights and days, the things they believe, the things that move them to pain and anger and the callous, idle cruelties that are yet undead. When I hear or read of a dog tortured to death, very vilely and foully, of some old horse driven to a broken back down a hill with an overloaded cart of corn, of rats captured and tormented with red-hot pokers in bothies, I have a shudder of disgust. But these things do not move me too deeply, not as the fate of the old-time Cameronian prisoners over there, three miles away in Dunnottar; not as the face of that ragged tramp who went by this afternoon; not as the crucifixion of the Spartacist slaves along the Appian Way. To me it is inconceivable that sincere and honest men should go outside the range of their own species with gifts of pity and angry compassion and rage when there is horror and dread among humankind. I am unreasonably and mulishly prejudiced in favour of my own biological species. I am a jingo patriot of planet earth: 'Humanity right or wrong!'

Particularly in Autumn. At noon I crossed a field off which the last of the stooks had been lifted and led captive away, the gaping stubble heads pushed through the cricks of clay, the long bouts of the binder wound and wheeled around the park, where the foreman had driven his team three weeks before. And each of those minute stubble stalks grew from seed that men had handled and winnowed and selected and ploughed and harrowed the earth to receive, and sown and tended and watched come up in the rains of Springs and the hot Summer suns – each and all of these – and out and beyond their kindred trillions in the other parks, up to the biggings of Upperhill there, and south through all the chave of the Howe to the black lands that start by Brechin and roll down the coast till they come to the richness of Lothian and the orchards of Blairgowrie. . . . This is our power, this the wonder of humankind, our one great victory over nature and time. Three million years hence our descendants out on some tremendous furrowing of the Galaxy, with the Great Bear yoked to The Plough and the wastes of space their fields, will remember this little planet, if at all, for the men who conquered the land and wrung sustenance from it by stealth and shrewdness and a savage and surly endurance. Nothing else at all may endure in those overhuman memories: I do not think there is anything else I want to endure.

The ricks loom tall and white in the moonlight about their yellow bosses: folk are loosening the heavy horses from the carts and leading them tramp, tramp across the cobbles of the close: with a scrape and clatter by the watertrough and a silence and then the sound of a slavering long, enjoyable long suction: I feel thirsty in sympathy with that equine delight of cool, good water in a parched mouth and throat. Then a light blinks through the cobwebs of the stable, an impatient voice says *Wissh!* and harvest is over.

Quiet enough here, because the very young and irresponsible are not here. But elsewhere, nights like this, up and down the great agricultural belts of Scotland, in and about the yards and the ricks, there is still some relic of the ancient fun at the last ingathering of the sheaves – still a genial clowning and drinking and a staring at the moon, and slow, steady childes swinging away to the bothies, their hands deep down in their pouches, their boots striking fire from the cobbles; still maids to wait their lads in the lee of the new-built stacks, and be cuddled and warm and happy against brown, dank chests, and be kissed into wonder on the world, and taste the goodness of the night and the Autumn's end. . . . Before the Winter comes.

To-morrow the potato harvests, of course. But somehow they are not real harvests, they are not truly of Autumn as is the taking in of the corn. It is still an alien plant, the potato, an intruder from that world of wild belief and wilder practice that we call the New, a plant that hides and lairs deep down in the midst of back-breaking drills. The corn is so ancient that its fresh harvesting is no more than the killing of an ancient enemy-friend, ritualistic, that you may eat of the flesh of the God, drink of his blood, and be given salvation and life.

SELECT BIBLIOGRAPHY OF MITCHELL'S WORKS

NON-FICTION

J. LESLIE MITCHELL, *Hanno: or the Future of Exploration: an Essay in Prophecy*, 1928.

LEWIS GRASSIC GIBBON, *Niger: the Life of Mungo Park*, 1934.

J. LESLIE MITCHELL, *The Conquest of the Maya*, 1934.

J. LESLIE MITCHELL and LEWIS GRASSIC GIBBON, *Nine Against the Unknown: a Record of Geographical Exploration*, 1934.

NOVELS

J. LESLIE MITCHELL, *Stained Radiance: A Fictionist's Prelude*, 1930.

J. LESLIE MITCHELL, *The Thirteenth Disciple, being Portrait and Saga of Malcolm Maudslay in his Adventure Through the Dark Corridor*, 1931.

J. LESLIE MITCHELL, *Three Go Back*, 1932.

J. LESLIE MITCHELL, *The Lost Trumpet*, 1932.

LEWIS GRASSIC GIBBON, *Sunset Song*, 1932.

J. LESLIE MITCHELL, *Image and Superscription: a novel*, 1933.

LEWIS GRASSIC GIBBON, *Cloud Howe*, 1933.

J. LESLIE MITCHELL, *Spartacus*, 1933.

J. LESLIE MITCHELL, *Gay Hunter*, 1934.

LEWIS GRASSIC GIBBON, *Grey Granite*, 1934.

LEWIS GRASSIC GIBBON, *A Scots Quair, a Trilogy of Novels: Sunset Song, Cloud Howe, Grey Granite*, 1946.

SHORT STORY COLLECTIONS

J. LESLIE MITCHELL, *The Calends of Cairo*, 1931.

J. LESLIE MITCHELL, *Persian Dawns, Egyptian Nights*, 1932.

MISCELLANY

LEWIS GRASSIC GIBBON and HUGH MACDIARMID, *Scottish Scene or the Intelligent Man's Guide to Albyn*, 1934.

NOTES

The notes in this edition are intended to serve the needs of overseas students as well as those of British-born users.

Page

1 *Bervie*: short form of Inverbervie, royal burgh on the Kincardine coast.

Tocherty: while some are fictitious, most of the placenames used by Mitchell in 'Smeddum', 'Greenden', 'Sim' and 'Clay' are those of places near his Bloomfield home – e.g. Auchindreich, Bervie Water, Drumlithie, Kinneff, Mondynes – but he also employs the places he created for *A Scots Quair*: the parish of Kinraddie (*Sunset Song*) and the weaving town of Segget (*Cloud Howe*).

2 *closet-bed*: or *box-bed*, bed with wooden sides and a roof and a door of two sliding or hinged panels.

3 *Stonehive*: one of the local forms of pronunciation of Stonehaven, county town of Kincardine.

4 *Howe*: Howe of the Mearns, a hill-girt basin in north Angus and Kincardine forming the north-eastern end of the Vale of Strathmore.

5 *Ag*: diminutive form of Agnes.

7 *Brechin*: royal burgh in the county of Angus.

9 *Mearns*: a division of the Celtic Province of Circhenn and the old name for what is now principally Kincardine.

12 *Mains*: the name given to the home farm of an estate.

Free Kirk: the Free Church of Scotland, well known for its fundamentalism and emphasis on godliness.

13 *old Pittendreich's*: farmers were commonly referred to by the name of their farm.

15 *There is a green hill far away* . . . : the first verse of the hymn by Cecil Frances Alexander (1823–95).

NOTES

24 *Boers:* the Dutch settlers who fought the British in the South African wars of 1880–1 and 1899–1902.

36 *'Eloi! Eloi! lama sabachthani?':* 'My God! My God! why hast thou forsaken me?' (St Matthew 27:46).

Mercat Cross: Market Cross (originally a cross or other sign set up where a market was to be held).

40 *El Kuds: Al-Quds,* or *Bait al-Maqdis,* Jerusalem.

Magdalene: Mary of Magdala, whose sins were forgiven by Christ (Luke 7:37–48).

box bed: see note to p. 2.

42 *Sanhedrin:* the supreme council and court at Jerusalem which condemned Christ to death.

61 *Kaltwasser:* Karl Kaltwasser (b. 1894), German historian.

62 *Maglemosian:* people of the transitional period between Palaeolithic and Neolithic, named after Maglemose in Denmark where traces of their culture were found.

Cro-Magnard: a type of man who has survived from an upper Palaeolithic culture to the present day. Named after Cro-Magnon in Dordogne, France, where the first skulls of the type were found.

Magdalenian: race of an upper Palaeolithic culture named after La Madeleine, a cave on the Vézère in France.

63 *Devil Stones:* pre-historic monoliths raised, in popular tradition, by the Devil. Also known as Druid Stones because they were used by the ancient priests who re-consecrated and adapted known places of worship to their own religious purposes.

Lewis: the island of Lewis in the Outer Hebrides.

64 *Pytheas:* Greek navigator of the fourth century B.C. who sailed the east coast of Britain.

Calgacus: one of the chief leaders of the Caledonians who were defeated at the battle of Mons Graupius in A.D. 84 by the Romans under Gnaeus Julius Agricola (37–93).

Kenneth MacAlpin: ninth-century ruler of Picts and Scots.

Normanized Kelt: a reference to the movement of Anglo-Normans to Scotland between 1114–1219. Many Scottish family names (e.g. Cumming, Lindsay, Sinclair) are of

French or Anglo-Norman origin.

65 *Dalriada:* founded in Argyll by the Dalriads of Ireland about A.D. 498.

66 *broch:* thick-walled circular fortress built by Early Iron Age farmers.

Columba: St Columba, Colum-cille or Colm (521–97), founded the monasteries of Derry and Durrow before quarrelling with the Irish king Diarmit. His defeat of the king at the battle of Culdremhene in 561 caused his excommunication and exile from his native land. He eventually went to the island of Iona where he founded a monastery in 563 and then set out with his followers to convert the Northern Picts. He later founded monasteries on the Pictish Mainland, the Orkneys and Western Isles.

John Knox: the principal leader of the Reformation in Scotland died in 1572.

Druid: priest of the ancient Celts of Britain, Gaul and Germany.

67 *Battle of Aberlemno:* in the Mearns about 1012 when the Danes were defeated by Malcolm II.

Duncan: Duncan I, slain by Macbeth in 1040.

James VI: (1566–1625), of Scotland from 1567, I of England from 1603.

68 *Malcolm Canmore:* Malcolm III, slain at Alnwick in 1093.

Princess Margaret: (c.1045–93), born in Hungary where her father was in exile. Said to have died on receiving news of her husband's death and was later canonised by Pope Innocent IV.

Mary the Unchaste: Mary, Queen of Scots (1542–87).

69 *Wyntoun:* Andrew of Wyntoun, (c.1350–c.1420), Scottish rhyming chronicler, author of *The Orygnale Cronykil of Scotland.*

Barbour: John Barbour (c.1316–96). *The Brus,* his narrative poem about the life and deeds of Robert the Bruce, was first printed in Edinburgh in 1571.

Blind Harry: (c.1470–92), Scottish minstrel who was born blind. His poem on Wallace runs to 11,861 lines.

William Wallace: Sir William Wallace, Walays or Wallensis, (c.1274–1305).

Cromwell: Oliver Cromwell (1599–1658), major English statesman and soldier, Protector of the Commonwealth of England, Scotland and Ireland from 1654 until his death.

Lincoln: sixteenth president of the United States of America, Abraham Lincoln (1809–65), regarded as the saviour of his country.

Lenin: Vladimir Ilyich Ulyanov (1870–1924), afterwards Lenin, Russian revolutionary and Marxist who inaugurated 'the dictatorship of the proletariat'.

Edward the First: (1239–1307). Buried in Westminster Abbey where a Latin inscription describes him as the 'Hammer of the Scots'.

John Richard Green: (1837–83), English historian. His innovatory and successful *Short History of the English People* (1874) was afterwards enlarged and re-published as *A History of the English People* (1877–80).

1 *Robert the Brus:* (1274–1329), Robert I of Scotland from 1306.

spiders: legend tells of a demoralised Robert the Bruce hiding in a cave. There he watched a spider endeavouring to spin a web and its repeated efforts despite many failures demonstrated to the king that he must try, try, and try again.

Lorne loons: at Dalry, on the Argyll and Perthshire border, Robert the Bruce was defeated in 1306 by John MacDougal, Lord of Lorne.

James the Fourth: (1473–1513), king of Scotland from 1488.

2 *Fifth James:* (1512–42), king of Scotland from 1513.

Henry VIII: (1491–1547). His many controversial deeds included the suppression of the monasteries.

3 *Cardinal Beaton:* David Beaton or Bethune (1494–1546), persecutor of the Protestants, was Archbishop of St Andrews at the time of his assassination.

Calvin: the Genevan religious reformer, John Calvin (1509–64).

5 *Second Charles:* Charles II (1603–85).

6 *Graham of Claverhouse:* John Graham of Claverhouse (c.1649–

89), 1st Viscount Dundee, was called 'Bonny Dundee', but was also known conversely as 'Bloody Claverse'.

77 *Darien:* the Isthmus of Darien, near Panama.

auld enemy: the English.

Fletcher of Saltoun: Andrew Fletcher (1655–1716), Scottish patriot who died in London.

Earl of Mar: John Erskine (1675–1732), known as 'Bobbing Joan' because of his frequent changes of allegiance.

Prince Charles Edward: Charles Edward Louis Philip Casimir Stewart (1720–88), called 'Bonnie Prince Charlie', the 'Young Pretender' and the 'Young Chevalier', who latterly assumed the title of Charles III of Great Britain and died in his birthplace of Rome.

80 *Siva:* also known as *Mahedeva*, destroyer and reproducer, the third god of the Hindu triad. ('Siva Plays the Game' was the title of Mitchell's winning entry in a short story competition in *T.P.'s and Cassell's Weekly* in 1924.)

81 *Azilian:* people of the Mesolithic culture, named after Mas D'Azil in France.

cave in Argyll: the Obanian cave-settlements on the Argyll coast were occupied by strand-loopers.

82 *Morlocks of Wells:* the race living in perpetual darkness underground and capturing the Eloi (the above-ground people) as food in the scientific romance *The Time Machine* (1895) by Herbert George Wells (1866–1946).

where he and his true love . . . : 'But me and my true love will never meet again' is a line from the song *The Bonnie Banks o' Loch Lomond.*

The Modern Scot: a quarterly Scottish Nationalist periodical first published in Dundee in 1930 which amalgamated with *Scottish Standard* in 1936 to form *Outlook.*

Adam Kennedy: pseudynom of John S. Buist.

The Mourners: apparently never appeared in book form, but Adam Kennedy's novel *Orra Boughs* (also printed in *The Modern Scot*) was published in a limited edition of thirty copies in 1930.

NOTES

83 *Douglasism: Social Credit,* by Clifford Hugh Douglas (1879–
    1952), was published in 1924. The author's idea of removing
    financial initiative from the hands of a minority and creating
    a system of social credit operating in a democratic economy
    appealed to many Scottish Nationalists and others because
    it appeared to offer a way to individual human freedom.
    Hugh MacDiarmid contributed an eulogy to Douglas in
    Scottish Scene, but Mitchell held a different view.

84 *Miss Wendy Wood:* writer, leader of The Scottish Patriots and
    editor of the nationalist periodical *Smeddum,* first published
    in 1938.

    Scone Stone: or Stone of Destiny, the ceremonial stone on which
    Scottish kings were enthroned in the Abbey of Scone was
    seized in 1296 by Edward I and placed in Westminster
    Abbey. In 1950 Mitchell's fantasy proved partly prophetic
    when three students removed the stone from Westminster.
    In 1951 the stone (or a reproduction) was deposited in the
    Abbey of Arbroath where, in 1320, the barons and clergy
    had declared the independence of their country in a letter
    (known as the Declaration of Arbroath) to the Pope.

    Compton Mackenzie: Sir Edward Montague Compton Mackenzie
    (1883–1972), born in West Hartlepool, novelist and writer
    who was made honorary chairman of the Scottish Nationalist
    Party in 1958. He dedicated his *Catholicism and Scotland*
    (1936) to the memory of 'J. Leslie Mitchell (Lewis Grassic
    Gibbon)'.

    St. Kilda: a remote island in the Outer Hebrides. The hopeless-
    ness of trying to sustain a viable community, and the misery
    of its inhabitants, eventually led to the evacuation of St
    Kilda in 1930.

    George Blake: (1893–1961), Glasgow-born novelist and writer.

    Duke of Montrose: called by some 'a tartan Tory', he joined in
    1933 with some members of the Cathcart (Glasgow) Unionist
    Party to found the Scottish Party which afterwards merged
    with the Nationalist Party to form the Scottish Nationalist
    Party in 1934.

Albyn: Scotland.

Maxton: James Maxton (1885–1946), Scottish politician, supporter of the Independent Labour Party and M.P.

R.M. Black: Robin McKelvie Black, editor of the Scottish Nationalist and Douglasite periodical *The Free Man,* first published in Edinburgh in 1932.

85 *ad lib.: ad libitum,* at pleasure (used in the sense of endless discourse).

ad nauseam: to produce sickness (to produce a feeling of disgust).

Braid Scots: Broad Scots, name given to the Scottish language.

86 *Josef Israel:* Josef Israels (1824–1911), Dutch painter and etcher who portrayed scenes from humble life.

Millais: Sir John Everett Millais (1829–96), English painter and woodcut designer.

87 *Christian Scientist:* adherent of the creed founded by Mary Baker Glover Eddy (1821–1910), an American who became minister in Boston of the Church of Christ, Scientist and whose *Science and Health with Key to the Scriptures* (1875) taught that disease is an illusion.

Glasgow Green: open-air site popular with orators.

Guy Aldred: Guy Alfred Aldred (b.1886), anti-parliamentary communist, editor of *The Commune,* prolific writer and propagandist.

St. Bakunin: Mikhail Bakunin (1814–76), Russian anarchist and revolutionary who believed that communism was an essential step towards anarchism.

Neanderthaler: man of a Palaeolithic species whose remains were found in a cave in the Neanderthal valley in Germany.

Homo Sapiens: the one existing species of man.

88 *National Party of Scotland:* in 1928 the Scottish Home Rule Association, the Scottish National Movement, the Scots National League and the Glasgow University Scottish Nationalist Association merged to form the Nationalist Party of Scotland with the objective of securing 'self-government for Scotland with independent national status within the British group of nations'. In 1934 the Nationalist

Party joined with the Scottish Party (founded in 1933) to form the Scottish Nationalist Party.

Ruth and Naomi: see Ruth 1:2-4.

Harry Lauder: Sir Harry Lauder (1870–1950), famous Scottish comedian and song-writer.

Baal: false god.

Manchukuo: puppet state established in the Manchurian Province of north-eastern China by the Japanese in 1932. Manchuria reverted to China in 1945.

90 *Ludovic Grant, writing . . . :* the quotation is taken from his article 'Which Culture?' in *The Free Man* Vol. II (new series) No. 41.

The Free Man: Scottish Nationalist and Douglasite periodical published in Edinburgh 1932–47.

Chichen-Itza: Chichén-Itzá, in the Yucatán, Mexico. Once a city of the Itzas, a powerful Maya nation, it is now a ruin. Mitchell's *The Conquest of the Maya* was published in the same year as this essay.

lion rampant: the yellow flag bearing a red Lion Rampant within a double tressure, flowered contrariwise, is the Royal Banner of the monarch of Scotland.

Brahmaputra: river rising in Tibet and entering the sea at the Bay of Bengal.

Heptarchians: people of the seven Anglo-Saxon kingdoms of East Anglia, Essex, Kent, Mercia, Northumbria, Sussex and Wessex supposedly subject from the sixth to the ninth century to government by seven persons.

91 *Bell o' the Brae:* an incident about 1297 when Wallace and his men attacked and defeated the English troops who then fled to nearby Bothwell in what is now Lanarkshire.

92 *Alan Porter:* Felix Alan Porter (1899–1942), English poet, critic and editor.

Bekhterev: Vladimir Mikhailovich Bekhterev (1857–1927), Russian neuropathologist.

Pavlov: Ivan Petrovich Pavlov (1849–1936), Russian physiologist who used dogs in his experimental studies of conditioned or acquired reflexes.

Bernard Shaw: George Bernard Shaw (1856–1950), Dublin-born critic, essayist, pamphleteer and major dramatist. He championed many causes including anti-vivisection.

93 *Melville:* Herman Melville (1819–91), American writer.

Typee: title of Herman Melville's first book (1846).

Joyce: James Augustine Aloysius Joyce (1882–1941), Dublin-born major writer.

Proust: Marcel Proust (1871–1922), major French novelist.

94 *Rabindranath Tagore:* (1861–1941), Indian poet and philosopher. He was the first Asiatic to receive the Nobel prize for literature.

95 *Eric Linklater:* (1899–1974), writer and novelist. Regarded as an Orcadian despite his Welsh birth. In 1935 he dedicated *The Lion and the Unicorn or What England has meant to Scotland* 'To the memory of Lewis Grassic Gibbon who asked me to write this book'.

ex cathedra: from the chair (i.e. authoritatively).

Hatter's Castle: (1931), the novel by A.J. Cronin.

House with the Green Shutters: towards the end of the nineteenth century Scottish writing had reached such a state of unreality that it became known as the Kailyard (cabbage-patch) school and *The House with the Green Shutters* (1901) by George Douglas Brown (1869–1902) is generally acknowledged as the first reaction and counterblast to the Kailyard. Conversely, Professor Douglas Young called Brown's book the 'leading novel of the "Stinkin Fush" school of Scottish literature'.

Dr. Cronin: Archibald Joseph Cronin (b.1896) abandoned the practice of medicine in 1930 to become a highly successful novelist.

Virginia Woolf: (1882–1941), English novelist.

96 *Strindberg:* Johan August Strindberg (1849–1912), Swedish dramatist, novelist and critic who was an exponent of many things at various times including, in his plays *Fadren* (1887) and *Fröken Julie* (1888), naturalistic drama.

Dr. Freud: Sigmund Freud (1856–1939), Austrian founder of psycho-analysis.

Paul Einzig: (b.1897), writer and economist.

Roy Campbell: Ignatius Roy Dunnachie Campbell (1901–57), South African poet and journalist of Irish and Scottish ancestry who was for a time a bullfighter in France.

Johnsonese: the heavy moralising and style of the essays of Samuel Johnson (1709–84), the English lexicographer, have rendered them almost unreadable to the contemporary eye.

Norman Douglas: George Norman Douglas (1868–1952), Scottish writer who spent most of his life in Italy.

97   *Joseph Conrad:* (1857–1924), Polish-born novelist who became a naturalised Briton in 1884.

Mr. Cunninghame Graham: Robert Bontine Cunninghame Graham (1852–1936), London-born Scottish author and politician who was in turn Liberal MP (1886–92), first honorary president of the Scottish Labour Party (1888) and first president of the Nationalist Party of Scotland (1928). In his youth he made the first of many visits to South America where he engaged in ranching until he succeeded to the family estate at Gartmore, Stirlingshire. His friends called him 'Don Roberto', the name given in his honour to the Argentinian city and the title of his biography (1937) by A.F. Tschiffely. He died in Buenos Aires, but was buried in Scotland.

Dr. James Bridie: pseudonym of Osborne Henry Mavor (1888–1951), Glasgow-born dramatist.

Edwin Muir: (1887–1959), Orkney-born major poet.

Dumas père: the French novelist and playwright Alexandre Dumas Davy de la Pailleterie (1802–70) was the grandson of a Haytian negress. The term père (father) is applied to Dumas to distinguish him from his natural son, Alexandre (1824–95), also a writer.

Dr. Charles Murray: (1864–1941), Scottish poet who wrote in the Donside dialect of Aberdeenshire.

Mr. W.H. Hamilton: William Hamilton Hamilton (b.1886) who rejected, in the introduction to his anthology *Holyrood: A Garland of Modern Scots Poems* (1929), the view that Scottish Calvinism dominated or discountenanced the arts in Scotland – a rejection not shared by Mitchell in his essay on religion in *Scottish Scene.*

Eden Philpotts: (1862–1960), Indian-born English novelist, poet and dramatist. His realistic novels chiefly dealt with Devonshire.

Tennyson: Alfred, 1st Baron Tennyson (1809–92), major English poet.

98 *Mrs. Naomi Mitchison:* (b.1897), became Lady Mitchison in 1964. *The Conquered* was published in 1923 and *Black Sparta* in 1928.

Lewis Grassic Gibbon: Mitchell's pseudonym, created to avoid confusing readers of his very different books published under his own name, was an adaptation of his mother's maiden name, Lilias Grassic Gibbon.

Dostoieffski: Fyodor Mikhailovich Dostoieffski (1821–81), Russian novelist.

Tolstoi: Count Leo Nikolayevich Tolstoi (1828–1910), Russian writer and philosopher.

Mr. Neil Gunn: Neil Miller Gunn (1891–1973), Caithness-born major novelist. *The Lost Glen* was published in 1932 and *Sun Circle* in 1933.

Mrs. Willa Muir: (b.1890), wife of Edwin Muir (see note to p. 97). Her novels *Imagined Corners* and *Mrs. Ritchie* were published in 1931 and 1933 respectively. In 1936 the dedication to her *Mrs. Grundy in Scotland* read 'This Book was Planned for the Delectation of LEWIS GRASSIC GIBBON and can only be dedicated instead, humbly and sorrowfully, to his memory'.

99 *John Buchan:* 1st Baron Tweedsmuir (1875–1940), Scottish author and statesman. His poetry anthology *The Northern Muse* was published in 1925.

Rider Haggard: Sir Henry Rider Haggard (1856–1925), English novelist.

NOTES

Sir Walter Scott: (1771–1832), Scottish poet and major novelist.

Marquis of Montrose: James Graham (1612–50), Scottish general.

Mrs. Catherine Carswell: (1879–1946), Glasgow-born writer. Her *Life of Robert Burns* was published in 1930 and *The Savage Pilgrimage: A Narrative of D.H. Lawrence* in 1932.

Mr. Middleton Murry: John Middleton Murry (1889–1957), British writer and critic whose book about D.H. Lawrence, *Son of Woman,* was published in 1931.

D.H. Lawrence: David Herbert Lawrence (1885–1930), English poet and novelist.

Hatter's Castle: was published in 1931, *Three Loves* in 1932 and *Grand Canary* in 1933.

Miss Mannin: Ethel Edith Mannin (b.1900), London-born novelist and writer.

Gilbert Frankau: (1884–1952), English novelist and poet.

Sir James George Frazer: (1854–1941), born in Glasgow.

Golden Bough: (1890). A rewritten version (1911–15) was published in twelve volumes.

Tylor: Sir Edward Burnet Tylor (1832–1917), English anthropologist.

The Men of Ness: was published in 1932, *Juan in America* in 1931 and *Magnus Merriman* in 1934.

Mark Twain: pseudonym of the American writer Samuel Langhorne Clemens (1835–1910). His *Tramp Abroad* was published in 1880.

Muriel Stuart: her *Christ at Carnival* was published in 1916.

Dante: Durante, afterwards Dante, Alighieri (1265–1321), major Italian poet.

Hugh MacDiarmid: principal pseudonym of Christopher Murray Grieve (1892–1978), born in Langholm, Dumfriesshire. Poet and polemical writer, the major figure of the Scottish Literary Renaissance, self-proclaimed anglophobe, founder-member of the Nationalist Party of Scotland, individualistic communist and Mitchell's collaborator in *Scottish Scene.* Mitchell dedicated *Grey Granite* (1934) to MacDiarmid who appeared in the novel as 'Hugo MacDownall'.

Lewis Spence: James Lewis Thomas Chalmers Spence (1874–1955), Scottish poet, author and anthropologist.

first of MacDiarmid . . . encountered: the poem quoted, 'Watergaw', was the first (although previously published anonymously) to appear under the name of Hugh MacDiarmid.

To Circumjack Cencrastus: was published in 1930.

Hymns to Lenin: Mitchell's reference is to *First Hymn to Lenin and other poems* (1931) and possibly to the limited edition in 1932 of *Second Hymn to Lenin and other poems,* re-published in 1935.

103 *'Time that has dinged doun castels . . .':* the first lines of 'The Queen's Bath-House, Holyrood'.

Elijah . . . Elisha: the prophet Elijah the Tishbite chose Elisha as his successor.

via terrena: way of the earth.

104 *James Barke:* (1905–58), Scottish writer who dedicated his *The End of the High Bridge* (1935) 'To Lewis Grassic Gibbon'. *The World his Pillow* was published in 1933 and *The Wild MacRaes* in 1934.

Donald Sinclair: Dòmhnall Mac na Ceàrdaich (1886–1933), Gaelic poet and dramatist.

Duncan Johnston: Donnachadh MacIain, born in Islay in 1881, Gaelic songwriter and poet.

John MacFadyen: Iain MacPhaidein, born in Mull in 1890, Gaelic poet.

Alasdair MacMhaighistir Alasdair: Alasdair Mac Mhaighstir Alasdair ('Alexander son of Master Alexander'), the Gaelic familiar address of Alexander MacDonald (Dòmhnall MacDhòmhnaill), Jacobite and major poet, born about 1690. Author of the first Scottish Gaelic vocabulary (1741), his first volume of poems *Ais-eiridh na Sean Chanain* ('The Resurrection of the Old Highland Language') was the first original work in Scottish Gaelic to be published (1751). He died in 1770.

Duncan Ban MacIntyre: Donnchadh Bàn Mac an t-Saoir (1724–1812), also known as Donnchadh Bàn nan Oran ('Fair-haired Duncan of the Songs'), major Scottish Gaelic poet who could neither read nor write and committed to memory some six thousand lines of his verse. Taken down from the poet's recital, his *Gaelic Songs* were first published in Edinburgh in 1768.

Alexander MacDonald: see *Alasdair MacMhaighistir Alasdair* above.

Ewan MacColl: Eoghan MacColla (1808–98), the Lochfyne poet. His first collection of poems and songs in Gaelic and English, *The Mountain Minstrel,* was published in 1836.

Young Pretender: see note to *Prince Charles Edward* on p. oo.

105 *Fionn MacColla:* pseudonym of Thomas Douglas Macdonald (1906–75).

Sic itur ad astra: such is the way to the stars.

106 *'Scotia Irredenta':* Scotland Unredeemed.

Kailyard: the nineteenth-century Scottish writers of the Kailyard (cabbage-patch) school can readily be identified by their sentimental, sugary and unrealistic misrepresentations of Scottish life. (See note to *The House with the Green Shutters* on p. oo).

Merse: the old name for the eastern border area of southern Scotland, especially Berwickshire.

Carse: alluvial river-side plain.

108 *Venriconian:* the *Venicones* were one of the four tribes recorded by the Greek geographer Claudius Ptolemaeus or Ptolemy (c.90–c.150) and others as occupying a territory which apparently lay southwards from Aberdeenshire to the Firth of Forth.

The Thirteenth Disciple: Mitchell's second novel, published in 1931.

Neolithic men: of the later Stone Age.

Mr. Chesterton: Gilbert Keith Chesterton (1874–1936), English critic, poet and novelist, was a convert to Roman Catholicism in 1922.

chelas: disciples.

109 *Kamtchatkan:* the Kamchatka peninsula in north-east Siberia.

135

110 *voice of the turtle:* see The Song of Solomon, 2:12.

   sovkholz: state farm in the USSR.

111 *aristos:* aristocrats.

   Green International: word-play on Red International, the third
      (1919–43) of four Internationals, or worldwide communist
      organisations. The first, called the International Working-
      men's Association, was founded by Kam Marx in 1864.

   Spartacus: Thracian shepherd and robber who was captured
      and sold as a slave. In 72 BC he escaped and led a slave
      rebellion, overcoming several Roman armies and laying
      waste much of Italy before his defeat and death in 71 BC.
      He was the subject of Mitchell's eighth novel (1933).

114 *Tyrian:* red or purple, like the dye once prepared at Tyre
      on the Phoenician coast.

   'God and a' his gang . . .': the third verse of 'Crowdieknowe'.

115 *Sun Circles:* standing stone circles which may have been used
      by an agricultural (as opposed to pastoral) society to deter-
      mine the seasons.

   Alexander: Alexander the Great (356–323 BC).

   Jaxartes: the river on whose banks Alexander the Great over-
      threw the Scythians in 329 BC.

   box-cart: cart to which additional boards could be fixed to
      increase its height and capacity.

116 *Fray Bentos:* named after the Uruguayan town, the brand
      name of a corned beef first marketed in 1899.

117 *Spenglerian cycle:* the German writer Oswald Spengler (1880–
      1936) argued in his *Untergang des Abedlandes* (1918–22) that
      all civilisations or cultures are subject to the same cycle of
      growth and decay because of a predetermined 'historical
      destiny'.

118 *Gilbert White:* (1720–93), English clergyman and naturalist,
      author of the classic *Natural History and Antiquities of Selborne*
      (1789).

   H.J. Massingham: Harold John Massingham (1880–1952),
      English writer who had a dominant interest in the study of
      nature.

119 *Cameronian prisoners:* disciples of the tenets of the extreme Covenanting leader Richard Cameron (1648–80).

Dunnottar: Castle, now a ruin, near Stonehaven in Kincardine. In the 'Killing Time' (1685–87) about two hundred Covenanters were imprisoned ankle-deep in mud in a Dunnottar vault where many of them died.

Appian Way: Appia Via, a Roman military road running from Rome to Capua, and later continued to Beneventum and Brudusium, begun about 312 BC by Appius Claudius.

'Humanity right or wrong!': the toast given by Stephen Decatur (1779–1820) at Norfolk, Virginia, in 1816 included the phrase 'our country, right or wrong'.

GLOSSARY

Because there are variations in the meaning and spelling of many Scottish words, some of the explanations given here are appropriate only to the context in which the words are used.

a': all
a-be: alone
abide: suffer
ae: one
afeared: frightened
afore: before
agley: astray
aiks: oaks
ailed: troubled
ails: troubles
alow: below
alowe: aflame
antrin: strange
atween: between
aught: anything
auld: old
awful: very much
ay: yes
aye: always
ayont: beyond
back: ago
backerty-gets: backwards
bade: stayed
bairn: child
bass: door-mat
been ta'en: dead, died
ben: through

bents: hill-slopes
bide: stay
biggings: buildings
billies: lads
billy: lad
birling: swirling
birn: load
bit: small, little, puny; bit of a; morsel, piece, scrap, little bit
bit and pringled: 'cut and polished'
blab: tell
black affronted: thoroughly ashamed
blash: deluge
bleezin': blustering
blether: nonsensical talk
body: person
bonny: pretty, beautiful
bosses: ventilation openings in corn or hay stacks
bothy: dwelling-hut for farm servants
bout: extent of land mown straightforwardly
braes: hillsides

braid: broad
braw: fine, handsome
bree: liquor
breech-clout: breech-cloth
breeks: breeches, trousers
brig: bridge
britchens: part of harness which passes round the rear of a horse
Broo: (bureau) Labour Exchange
brose: oatmeal mixed with boiling water or milk and seasoned with butter or salt
brosy: sluggish
buirdly: stalwart, well-made
bursary: scholarship
by her lone: on her own
byre: cowhouse
cam: came
canna: cannot
cannily: carefully, craftily
canny: cautious
carrying: pregnant
castels: castles
cawing: calling (of birds, usually of crows)
chave: toil
chaving: toiling
childe: fellow
chirked: chirped, made a grating sound
chitterin': trembling
claik: tattle
clanging: clinging
clorted: besmeared

close: alley
clour: blow
clucking: broody
coarse: hard, bad
coddled: pampered
coldrife: very cold
coling: putting into haycocks
contemner: condemner
cookies: buns
cottar house: farm labourer's cottage or house
coulter: iron cutter at front of plough
couped: capsized, overturned, knocked down
couthy: agreeable
crack: chat
creash: greasy person
cricks: cracks
croft: small farm, small piece of arable land
crouns: crowns
crow: tickling sensation
daddling: fondling
daft: foolish
daftie: half-witted person
dander: stroll
dawtie: pet
deave: stupefier
dee'd: died
den: dell
diamant: diamond
dickie: false shirt-front
dight: rub
dinged: knocked, cast
dirt: rubbish, worthless persons

dishclouts: dishcloths
dominie: schoolmaster
dottlet: confused
douce: gravely
doun: down
dour: stubborn, unyielding
dowp: backside
dram: glass of whisky
dreich: dreary
drummle: muddiness, confusion; beat, murmur
drummlet: troubled
dumb-foundered: astounded, *taken aback*
dyke: wall of stone or turf
eirde: earth; earth-house
eldritch: unearthly
eyen: eyes
fa': fall
fair: fairly, certainly; have to; certain, quite
fairely: wonder; with wonder
fairlies: wonders, curiosities, novelties
fairly: certainly
famisht: famished
fash: bother
feared: frightened, afraid
fee: wage, job
fee'd: employed, paid
feeing: working for wages, taking a fee for work
feered: frightened, afraid
fegs: faith (used as an oath or exclamation of surprise)
feint: not, nothing

fell: very, exceedingly
felly: fellow
fettle: condition
feuch: an exclamation of disgust
fine: very good
finisht: finished
fleer: ogle
flit: removal
floures: flowers
flyting: scolding
forbye: in addition, as well as
forenicht: the early part of the night after twilight
frere: brother, friend
fuff: puff
fusionless: feeble
gait: way
galluses: trouser braces
galumphed: danced heavily
gang: go
gant: gape
ganting: yawning
garred: made
gawk: vacant stare
gear: possessions
gey: very, rather
gied: gave
girned: complained
girning: nagging, complaining
give's: give me
glaur: mud
gley: squint
glimmer: faint light, blink
glister: thin covering of sleet,

snow or ice; glitter

glowered: scowled

go: energy

goodson: son-in-law

gowk: cuckoo, fool

gowked: stared

graip: farm or garden fork with three or four iron prongs

grat: wept

'greed: agreed

greet: weep

grumphed: grunted

guff: smell, savour

gurling: swirling, rolling

guttering: full of puddles or gurgling, running water

habber: nonsensical talk

habbered: stammered

hacking: broken coughing

hae: have

haggis: the minced heart, liver and lungs of the sheep, mixed with oatmeal, onions, pepper, salt and suet, and cooked in a sheep's stomach or maw

halds: holds

half-minded: half-noticed

hame: home

hams: thighs

happed: covered

happing: enveloping

hapt: wrapped

hash: mess

haugh: low, level ground

beside a stream or river

heuch: hook

hie: high

hind: farm servant

hirpling: limping

hoast: cough

hold out: make way towards

hoose: house

hoots: an exclamation of irritation

hove: heaved

howe: hollow, hollow space

howlet: owlet

ilk: same kind, same nature

ill: disagreeable; harm

ill-getted: ill-begotten

ill-ta'en: bad-tempered

ingle-neuk: fireplace corner

intil: into

intilt: into it

jaloose: guess, suspect

joskin: farm servant

keek: peep

ken: know

kenned: knew

kent: knew

kirk: church

kittle up: liven up

kittled: born

kye: cattle

laired: layered

lang: long

laplaplap: rhythmic lapping sound

laverock: lark

leathering: punishing with a

leather tawse

let on: made known

letten: left

letten a-be: left alone

ley: grassland

licht: light

lift: sky

like: kind; probably

limner: roguish girl

lithe: shelter

lone: alone

loon: boy, fellow

loosed: unharnessed

loosened: unharnessed,
   stopped work

losh: lord (used as an
   exclamation of surprise)

loup: leap

louped: jumped

lour: lurk

lowe: flame, blaze

lug: ear

lum: chimney

Ma: mother

ma: my

mannie: man

manse: official house of a
   minister in Scotland

mart: market

maun: must

meat: food

meck: halfpenny

meikle: great, big, large

Mem: madam

midden: dung-hill

mighty: an exclamation of

surprise

min: man

minded: remembered,
   reminded

minding: remembering

mirk: murk

moiled: laboured hard

moonlight flit: night-time
   decampment to avoid
   detection

morn: morning; *the morn:*
   tomorrow morning

mouser: moustache

mowed: mouthed

muck out: clean out

nae: no

nane: none

near: nearly, just about

neb: nose

nicht: night

nichtgoon: nightgown

nickum: mischievous boy

nieve: fist, closed hand

nip: small glass of whisky

no: not

nout: cattle

oatcake: thin hard dry cake
   made with oatmeal

oe: youngest

on the go: on the move,
   working

on-ding: onset, attack

orra man: odd-job man

o't: of it

outby, outbye: outside

paiched: panted; sighed

heavily

palavers: pratings

park: grass-field

pawky: shrewd

peesies: lapwings

peewit: lapwing

plaid: blanket

plashed: splashed

plashing: splashing

pleiter: mess

pleitering: messing about

ploy: escapade, employment

pluffer: pea-shooter

pootsy: sweetheart, young girl

porridge: dish made by slowly stirring oatmeal in boiling water

press: cupboard

prig: plead

pringled: fine, 'polished'

puddock: frog

quean: girl

quiet: quieten

raxed: reached

redding: clearing

ree: sty

reek: smoke

rickle: heap

rig: space between furrows in a field

right: thoroughly, very

rive: tear

roup: auction-sale

rouped: sold up by auction

rousting: rousing

rumblet: rumbled

sall: shall

sappy: soft and simple

sark-like: gown-like

schiltrouns: squadrons

schlorich: wet mess

scoriate: scorch, burn

scoured: scrubbed

see: attend

seep: ooze

shackle-bone: wrist-bone

shammle: shamble

sharn: dung

sheeny: Jew

shelvins: boards used to heighten the sides of a cart to increase its capacity

shoggling: tottering

sholtie: pony

shoon: shoes

showd: sway

sin': since

skellacht: scattered

skelped: struck

skeugh: twisted

skirl: shriek

slabbering: slobbering

sleeked: crafty, cunning

smeddum: mettle, spirit

smokies: smoked haddocks

snibbed: bolted, closed

snicker: snigger

sniftering: snuffling

sonsy: happy, pleasant

soss: wet, dirty mess

sossing: working in dirt

sough: sigh

southron: southern

speak: talk

speir: ask

spunk: match

stammy-gastered: flabber-
gasted

stanes: stones

stan's: stands

steading: farm buildings

steeking: clenching

steer: commotion, bustle,
fuss

sticks: pieces of furniture

stirks: yearling cattle

stite: nonsense

stitering: stumbling

stock: useless person

stook: bundles of corn
sheaves set upright and
leaning against each other
to dry in the fields

stooking: making stands of
corn sheaves

stots: young steers

stour: dust

sumph: simpleton

swack: supple, active

swash: swish

swede: swede turnip

sweetie: sweet, sweetmeat

sweir: reluctant, lazy, loth

sweirty: laziness

swink: labour

swivel-trees: cross-pieces of a
plough

syne: then; ago

ta'en: taken

ta'en back: taken aback

ta'en no ill: come to no harm

taik: saunter

tailer: tool for cutting off
turnip roots

tashed: exhausted

tattie-shaws: leaves and stems
of potatoes

term: Whitsunday or
Martinmas

thae: those

thocht: thought

thole: bear, suffer

thrashen: thrashed

through hand: under
examination

tink: tinker, gypsy

tint: lost

tirred: stripped

tompions: tampions, nappies

topper: first-class, excellent
person or thing

tosh: rubbish

toun: farm; town

toures: towers

trauchle: drudgery, hard
work

trig: neat

tykes: curs

unchancy: risky

unco: extreme, uncommonly

unco-like: strange

undighted: untidied

unsteeking: unclenching

GLOSSARY

wabble: wobble

wame: stomach

water-gaw: part of a rainbow appearing on the horizon

wee: small

weet: wet

well-happed: well-covered

well-tacked: strongly hobnailed

wha: who

wheeber: whistle

whirlimagig: turn of fortune

whirlimagigs: whimsical, fanciful ornaments

whisht: hush

whisp: swish, rustle

whit: white

whoom: roar

wi': with

wissh: hush; a call to horses to turn right

wynds: narrow lanes

yavil: field lying a second year without being cropped or sown

Yid: Jew

yon: that

yow-trummle: 'ewe-tremble', a spell of cold weather in early summer supposedly chilling sheep